# Leadership in Action

## How Effective Directors Get Things Done

*Paula Jorde Bloom*

# NEW HORIZONS

EDUCATIONAL CONSULTANTS AND LEARNING RESOURCES

LAKE FOREST, ILLINOIS 60045-0863

Printed in the United States of America

**Library of Congress Cataloging-in-Publication Data**

Bloom, Paula J.
    Leadership in action : how effective directors get
things done / Paula Jorde Bloom
    p. cm. – (The director's toolbox : a management)
series for early childhood administrators)
    Includes bibliographical references.
    ISBN 0-9621894-7-2

    1. Early childhood education – United States –
Administration. 2. Educational leadership – United
States. 3. School personnel management – United States.
4. Early childhood educators – United States   I. Title.
II. Series.

    LB2822.6.B56 2003              372.12
                                   QBI33-1574

# NEW HORIZONS

Educational Consultants and Learning Resources
P.O. Box 863
Lake Forest, Illinois 60045-0863
(847) 295-8131
(847) 295-2968 FAX
newhorizons4@comcast.com

Books in **The Director's Toolbox Management Series** are available at quantity discounts for use in training programs. For information on bulk quantity rates or how to purchase a **Trainer's Guide** for this book, contact the publisher.

*Illustrations* – Marc Bermann
*Design* – Stan Burkat

# CONTENTS

# Chapter

1. **Leadership—Defining the Elusive** .................................................1
   - Leadership Roles .................................................2
   - Leadership Tasks and Functions..............................3
   - Leadership Skills and Competencies .......................5
   - Leadership Traits and Dispositions.........................6
   - Leadership as a Personal Style ..............................7
   - The Context of Early Childhood Leadership ..............8
   - The Good News—Leadership Ability Is Not Static .............11

2. **Leadership as a Way of Thinking** ..............................................13
   - Leadership as the Exercise of Influence ...........................13
   - Leadership as an Expression of Your Values........................19
   - Leadership as a Statement of Your Hopes and Dreams ........27

3. **The Starting Point—Know Thyself** ..............................................33
   - Which Leaders Have Inspired You or Disappointed You? ......34
   - Which Traits Define Your Leadership Style? ........................36
   - How Effective Do You Feel in Your Leadership Role?............38
   - What Image Do You Project?....................................39
   - What Are Your Assumptions About People? ........................40
   - What Is Your Work Orientation?....................................42
   - What Are Your Self-Expectations? ...................................45
   - Do You Regularly Seek Feedback From Others? .................47

4. **Becoming a Facilitative Leader** ...............................................51
   - Creating Connections ...................................................51
   - Shaping Expectations...................................................55
   - Expanding Perspectives .................................................60
   - My Commitment to Action .................................................64

**5.** **Bumper Stickers to Live By** .................................................67
- "Quality Is a Moving Target" .............................................67
- "Different Strokes for Different Folks" ..............................69
- "Don't Get Stuck in the Muck" ..........................................71
- "Simplicity Is Power" .......................................................72
- "Keep That Duct Tape Handy" ...........................................73
- "The Whole Is Greater Than the Sum of Its Parts" ..............76
- "It's the Little Things" .....................................................77
- "Laughter is the Shortest Distance Between Two People" ....78
- "Dedication Doesn't Have to Mean Deadication" ................79
- "You Can't Please All the People All the Time" .................81

**6.** **What Does it Mean to Walk the Talk?**.........................................83
- Striving for Authenticity....................................................83
- Living Your Personal Code of Ethics ..................................85
- Thinking About Your Successor ..........................................88

**7.** **A Final Word** ...............................................................93

**For Further Reading** .............................................................95

**Appendices** ........................................................................99
- **A.** Beliefs and Values Questionnaire ....................................101
- **B.** Multi-Rater Leadership Assessment ..................................103
- **C.** Collaboration Questionnaire...........................................108

# About the Author

Paula Jorde Bloom holds a joint appointment as Director of the Center for Early Childhood Leadership and Professor of Early Childhood Education at National-Louis University in Wheeling, Illinois. She received her baccalaureate degree from Southern Connecticut State University and her master's and Ph.D. degrees from Stanford University. Paula has taught preschool and kindergarten, designed and directed a child care center, and served as administrator of a campus laboratory school. She is a frequent keynote speaker at state, national, and international early childhood conferences and serves as a consultant to professional organizations and state agencies. Dr. Bloom is the author of numerous articles and several widely read books, including *Workshop Essentials*, *Circle of Influence*, *Living and Learning with Children*, *Avoiding Burnout*, *A Great Place to Work*, *Making the Most of Meetings*, and *Blueprint for Action*.

# Acknowledgements

Many people have influenced my thinking about the characteristics of effective leadership. Some of them were amazingly competent and inspirational individuals who transformed ordinary workplaces into exciting and vibrant learning communities. Others were astoundingly incompetent and self-absorbed individuals who alienated people and left their organizations in shambles. Both good and bad have reinforced for me the importance of strong leadership, especially in human service organizations.

On a personal level, I am indebted to my colleagues at the Center for Early Childhood Leadership for the opportunity to talk about, try out, and reflect on the principles shared in this book. In preparing the manuscript, I received wonderful advice from Jill Bella, Karla Berra, Eileen Eisenberg, Teri Talan, Cory Roberts Eisenberg, and Doug Clark. I am especially indebted to my husband, Darrell, for his inspiration on this topic. He continues to be the best example I know of a truly facilitative leader. Finally, thanks Catherine Cauman for working magic on my words with her careful editing.

# CHAPTER 1

# Leadership—
# Defining the Elusive

If you've browsed the business and management section of your local Barnes and Noble bookstore lately, no doubt you've noticed the flood of new titles on the topic of leadership. From Hans Finzel's best seller *The Top Ten Mistakes Leaders Make* to Ken Blanchard's motivational *Gung Ho!* the gurus in business, industry, and education are tripping over one another to extol the virtues of strong leadership. Some authors have taken the patron saints approach with titles like *Jesus—CEO* and *Moses on Management*. Others probe leadership from the inside out—an MRI approach—with catchy titles like *Leading Minds, Leading with Soul*, and *The Heart of the Leader*. Still others whet our leadership appetite with clever titles like *Who Moved My Cheese?* and *Fish!* Finally, some books, like Harvey Mackay's *Swim with the Sharks*, focus on the skills high-performing leaders need to outsmart their competition and keep their body parts intact.

Without question, strong leadership is an essential ingredient in any thriving organization. Leaders transform intentions into action. Despite the volumes that have been written on the topic, though, leadership remains an elusive concept for many early childhood administrators. The examples and case studies that fill the pages of popular leadership texts are often not relevant in the world of early care and education. This has made it difficult for early childhood directors to apply the important lessons of leadership from other disciplines to the work they do every day. *Leadership in Action—How Effective Directors Get Things Done* fills this void.

This book dispels two myths. First, that leadership is the domain of corporate CEOs, heads of state, and those with lofty titles overseeing legions of worker bees. Leadership *is* the business of every center director. It is one of the strongest predictors of high-quality early childhood programming. The second myth this book dispels is that there is one best leadership style all directors should emulate. Leadership is like pantyhose; one size does *not* fit all.

This chapter provides an overview. It examines leadership from five perspectives: leadership as a role, leadership tasks and functions, leadership as a repertoire of skills and competencies, leadership traits and dispositions, and leadership style. It concludes with a look at leadership in the context of early childhood education and the link between effective leadership and program quality. In later chapters you'll learn how you can apply the lessons of leadership in your own center.

A leader is someone you choose to follow to a place you wouldn't go by yourself.

*Joel Barker*

The target audience for *Leadership in Action*, like all the books in the Director's Toolbox Management Series, is early childhood administrators of center-based programs. But the concepts and ideas presented are clearly relevant to all who work in the field of early childhood. Indeed one of the dominant themes in this book is that effective early childhood programs cultivate leadership at all levels of the organizational chart. So leadership is not *your* business only, it is *everyone's* business.

## Leadership Roles

The term *leadership* evokes images of great men and women—Winston Churchill, John F. Kennedy, Eleanor Roosevelt, Martin Luther King Jr., Susan B. Anthony, Nelson Mandela—powerful, dynamic individuals who have led nations, inspired armies, and shaped history. Sadly, however, we have seen too often that many in leadership roles fail to live up to the expectations of their office or position. Presidents, corporate CEOs, and revered church leaders have been forced to step down from their lofty posts because of unethical or illegal conduct, their personal reputations tarnished and their organizations or institutions weakened. It seems the more esteemed the roles, the more disappointed we are when the ones holding such leadership positions do not live up to our expectations for moral conduct.

The titles and role descriptors of individuals in early childhood leadership positions are as varied as the field itself. How we describe leadership roles in part depends on how wide we cast our net. When we view leadership from the perspective of a preschool or child care center, some of the more common designators are administrator, director, principal, education coordinator, site manager, supervisor, and lead teacher.

But leadership can also be viewed from a much broader context if we consider individuals who, by the nature of their work, influence social and public policy and key issues facing the field. They may help advance early childhood scholarship and best practices through their research and writing, or they may challenge the status quo by advocating for change in policies and resource allocation. These individuals hold positions in professional and civic organizations, corporations, philanthropic foundations, federal and state agencies, institutions of higher education, and social service agencies. They have roles and job titles like child advocate, legislator, professor, policy analyst, agency executive director, resource and referral specialist, multi-site coordinator, and regional manager.

While leadership in this broader context is essential for helping to professionalize the field of early childhood, the examples and case studies included in this book are drawn predominantly from the work of directors whose job it is to provide service directly to children and families. The role of

B eing *the* leader does not make you a leader.

*Thomas Gordon*

directing an early childhood program is certainly one of the most rewarding in the human service professions. It is also among the most challenging, requiring stamina, the ability to juggle competing demands, and finesse in managing multiple relationships simultaneously. Most early childhood administrators carry out their roles in environments that are relentlessly underresourced. Any veteran in the role will confirm that it takes more than passion to be successful in the job.

## Leadership Tasks and Functions

Regardless of how narrow or broad one's perspective is in defining the role of a leader, the essential tasks and functions of an early childhood leader fit the definition—to inspire, to inform, to motivate, and to serve as a symbol for the collective identity of a group. Much of the literature in organizational theory refers to leadership as the exercise of influence; the use of power and position to prod, provoke, and persuade people to take a particular course of action. While the traditional pyramid structure of authority still exists in many early childhood programs, this model is giving way to more collaborative approaches of shared leadership.

Today the most enlightened directors of early childhood programs define *leading* as the process of influencing others to achieve mutually agreed-upon goals rather than coercing, controlling, or manipulating people to achieve desired outcomes. We'll dig deeper into the philosophy and values supporting this approach in Chapter 2.

**Leadership versus management.** The literature often differentiates between leadership functions and managerial functions. Leadership functions relate to the broad view of helping an organization clarify and affirm values, set goals, articulate a vision, and chart a course of action to achieve that vision. Like an artist, a leader paints the picture, creating the images of what an organization could be. A leader's job is to create a healthy tension between the current reality and an imagined ideal.

Managerial functions relate to the orchestration of tasks and establishment of systems to attain a vision. Planning, budgeting, organizing, and staffing are just some of the management functions that directors oversee. Some writers clarify the distinction between leadership and managerial functions as the difference between effectiveness and efficiency—leaders do the right things; managers do things right.

Leadership is often the capricious mixture of the trivial and the titanic.

## Two Sides of Early Childhood Administration

| Leadership | Management |
|---|---|
| Wants to do the right things | Wants to do things right |
| Concerned with effectiveness | Concerned with efficiency |
| Asks,<br>"What tasks do I want to accomplish?" | Asks,<br>"How can I best accomplish this task?" |
| Focuses on relationships | Focuses on rules and policies |
| Spends time on establishing a vision and seeking opportunities | Spends time on planning, organizing, and creating systems |
| Willing to take risks | Seeks stability |
| Thinks long range | Thinks short term |
| Stresses adaptive change | Supports the status quo |
| Motivates and inspires | Implements the work plan |
| Develops new alternatives and approaches | Establishes procedures and allocates resources |

Managers are often observed doing the wrong thing well.

*Warren Bennis*

Because of the relatively flat organizational structure of most early childhood programs, the tidy distinction between leadership and management functions that might be apparent in other organizational settings seldom exists in early childhood settings. Effective center directors are leaders providing vision and inspiration, as well as managers orchestrating the implementation of policies and procedures.

The goals and outcomes of early childhood programs also differ from traditional corporate indicators of success. Rather than defining units of output or bottom-line profits in a competitive environment, the organizational goals of early childhood leaders revolve around abstract notions like quality of service, which are more difficult to measure in quantitative terms. In child care settings, goals and desired outcomes are people oriented rather than product oriented.

**Directors' developmental progression.** My own research confirms there is a developmental progression of directors' focus of attention as it relates to the twin concepts of management and leadership. When directors first assume their administrative role, they tend to focus more on management issues, the nitty-gritty technical aspects of getting a program to run smoothly. Their temporal focus is on the immediate—what do they need to do here and now, today and tomorrow.

As confidence and a sense of self-efficacy in the role increase, directors' focus of attention becomes more diffuse. Concern broadens to include a greater emphasis on the leadership functions of vision building and systems change. Master directors—those seasoned high-performing individuals who administer early childhood programs—are capable of focusing on the present and the future simultaneously as they construct bridges to move their organization from where it is to where it needs to be.

## Leadership Skills and Competencies

Leadership can also be viewed as a repertoire of generic skills that promote effective program operations. The attraction of viewing leadership from this behavioral perspective is that it broadens our frame of reference. It means that one need not be in a specific leadership position to demonstrate effective leadership. The technical, human, and conceptual skills that define effective leadership can be categorized into four areas:

**Communication skills.** In both writing and speaking, effective leaders are able to synthesize complex information and communicate that information cogently and succinctly to different audiences. They are persuasive advocates for their cause and know how to explain issues with clarity and eloquence.

**Decision-making and problem-solving skills.** Effective leaders know how to work with others to isolate and define problems, weigh creative alternatives in solving those problems, and then take appropriate and timely action to implement needed changes.

**Interpersonal skills.** Effective leaders know how to motivate and energize others to pursue common aims. They are empathic listeners, sensitive to differing points of view, and they appreciate diversity as an organizational asset. They know how to manage the expectations of diverse stakeholders as well as negotiate differences before conflict erupts.

**Organizational skills.** Effective leaders know how to prioritize their time and are proactive in planning and anticipating the future. They are trend watchers who seek and sort out pertinent data that is important to the future of their organization. They have the ability to translate broad goals into concrete objectives and identify the resources needed to accomplish different tasks. And they know how to set up evaluation systems to monitor personal and organizational performance.

## Leadership Traits and Dispositions

For decades organizational theorists have debated the question of whether leaders are born or made. In other words, how much of leadership behavior can be attributed to innate personal traits and dispositions and how much is learned through training and experience. Research has shown only a weak association between personal characteristics such as voice quality, height, mannerisms, and general appearance and promotion to leadership roles.

There are, however, a few personal traits and dispositions that have been found to be more predictive of leadership success. Effective leaders exhibit passion about their cause and a tenacious focus in the pursuit of their goals. As a group they are generally risk takers, willing to take an unpopular stance. They are also achievement oriented, setting high but realistic goals for themselves and their organizations. They rely on both logic and intuition to make decisions and are unequivocal in the principles, beliefs, and values that guide their behavior. They recognize their strengths as well as their limitations, and they engage in objective introspection. In other words, they know themselves well.

Recent research on emotional intelligence also provides insight into the traits that predict successful leaders. Emotional intelligence (EI) is the capacity to understand and manage one's own emotions and those of others. While general intellect and cognitive skills (particularly big-picture thinking and long-range vision) are important in the leadership equation, the competencies that distinguish outstanding leaders at higher levels in an organization are those most associated with emotional intelligence.

Daniel Goleman, a pioneer in research on emotional intelligence, says that good leaders ignite our passion and inspire the best in us. When we try to explain why these leaders are so effective, we speak of strategy, vision, and powerful ideas. But the reality, Goleman believes, is more primal—great leaders work through our emotions. They know how to connect with our inner needs, particularly our need to be validated. This is good news because emotional intelligence competencies are not innate talents, but learned abilities.

O f course all leaders are born. I've yet to meet one that came into the world any other way!

*John Maxwell*

## Leadership as a Personal Style

The way leaders put into practice their repertoire of skills to carry out the tasks and functions of their job is their unique leadership style. We can think of leadership style as the defining thumbprint of a person's interaction with others to achieve the goals of an organization. The thumbprint metaphor is apt because it underscores the obvious—there is no one best style when it comes to leadership. Some effective leaders are charismatic and outgoing; others are quietly influential. Some are fast paced and action oriented; others are more reflective and deliberate.

You can think of your leadership style as the way you express your management philosophy through communication patterns, work preferences, general behaviors, and interactions with others. One of the earliest conceptions characterizes leadership style by where it falls on a continuum from *autocratic* to *laissez-faire*, depending on how much the leader involves or trusts subordinates to define and carry out their respective tasks. But this concept of leadership style has been discounted in recent years as too simplistic.

A more popular concept, contingency theory, defines leadership style as situational. Within this framework the effective leader can adapt his or her behavior according to the nature of the task at hand and the maturity and experience of the individuals who need to carry it out. This concept of leadership is attractive because it recognizes that the contextual factors of the organization influence the dynamics of human interactions. Individuals with a rigid, fixed style may be thwarted in their attempts to achieve desired outcomes. Effective leadership demands ongoing reassessment and realignment of goals, depending on the changing context of the work environment.

Many contemporary views of leadership focus on the central role of leaders as decision makers and problem solvers, highlighting the importance of participatory management and collaborative decision-making processes. Total Quality Management (TQM) is an example of such an approach. It stresses the importance of a leadership style that encourages an environment of openness and respect where employees closest to problems are empowered to identify strategies and possible solutions to pressing organizational issues.

**Transformational leadership.** Perhaps the most popular conceptualization of leadership style during the past decade emphasizes the transformational nature of the leadership role. Transformational leaders focus on energizing and engaging others to pursue common goals. They help generate awareness of the broader vision of the organization and work to support others in achieving higher levels of ability and potential. This means expanding people's perspectives by helping them look beyond their own self-interest to the greater good of the organization.

A transformational style is often contrasted with a transactional style in which a leader focuses on creating a system of economic, political, and psychological incentives to reward successful performance. In other words, a transactional leader gives followers something they want in exchange for something the leader wants—a quid pro quo. This sets up a relationship of mutual dependence, a kind of psychological contract in which the contributions of both sides are acknowledged and rewarded.

Transactional and transformational leadership can be thought of as representing different points on the same leadership continuum. Thus a transformational approach does not necessarily replace a transactional approach but rather augments and expands its effects by uniting followers around collective goals that produce higher levels of performance than previously thought possible.

A move from a transactional to a transformational leadership style means rethinking relationships of power in an organization. Instead of top-down, hierarchical approaches to decision making and problem solving, it means moving toward greater involvement of staff in shaping program goals and decisions. Transformational leadership requires more risk and initiative on the part of directors because it rests on reciprocity with others in building and strengthening organizational norms and culture. Directors who embrace this style think of themselves as social architects of their early care and education programs who create and maintain values that promote a sense of community, equity, and shared power.

## The Context of Early Childhood Leadership

If you are a seasoned early childhood administrator, you have witnessed first-hand how the social, economic, and political changes during the past decade have fundamentally altered the scope and nature of early childhood services. In addition to growing demand, several trends have created challenges for early childhood leaders. Whether you administer a for-profit or nonprofit program, provide half-day or full-day services, are independent, agency affiliated, faith-based, or corporate sponsored, five trends, listed on page 9, have affected how you do business.

Administering an early childhood program is never easy, but the increasing complexity of the external environment has elevated the need for strong leadership in the director's role. Think of your own program for a moment, and reflect on how these five trends have impacted you and your staff. For example, consider the trend for greater accountability. My guess is that issues like accreditation, credentialing, tiered reimbursement, and documenting learning

## Five Trends Impacting Early Childhood

1. **Emphasis on quality and accountability.** Greater demands for accountability are creating additional pressures for quality assurance evaluation and performance management systems that monitor, document, and report on center efficiency and quality of care.

2. **Federal devolution and legislation.** Welfare-to-work legislation and other federal initiatives are putting more parents into the workforce, resulting in many single parents employed in low-wage jobs. These newly employed adults not only add to the demand for quality child care but also require different kinds of support and service relationships.

3. **Heightened competition for qualified early childhood staff.** Staff turnover and retention issues continue to plague early childhood programs. Finding qualified staff who are caring, motivated, and committed to early childhood as a career remains a challenge.

4. **Pressure to integrate early childhood education into broader social service systems.** The social and human services environment within which many early childhood programs are operating requires stronger and more intensive linkages between social service delivery agencies and early care and education organizations.

5. **Greater competition for financial resources.** Competition for adequate levels of funding is demanding greater entrepreneurship and innovation. Funding systems, especially those linked to managed care, are negotiating contracts that pay on a "capitated basis"—they pay a fixed amount per client served—and these payments do not adequately cover the actual cost of providing care.

*Adapted from Renz, D. O. (2003, Summer). Developing leadership in the new millennium: Building capacity in the early care and education community. Kansas City, MO: Midwest Center for Nonprofit Leadership at the University of Missouri-Kansas City. Reprinted with permission.*

outcomes are now regular topics of conversation at your staff meetings. The nature and substance of your work in an early care and education program is clearly affected by how you, your board, and your staff respond to these accountability issues.

*I*'ve never seen a great program that didn't have a great director.

*Sue Bredekamp*

If you are like most directors, the funding and regulatory agencies with which you work now require more paperwork and documentation of program outcomes than ever before. Certainly no one disputes the need for quality assurance, but each new mandate imposed on your program or each new quality enhancement initiative you pursue on your own requires rethinking current practices and how best to achieve the desired outcomes.

Now think of your network of professional contacts—those stakeholders with whom you communicate regularly. Reviewing the sample stakeholder map for a typical early childhood administrator, think how your own personal stakeholder map might look.

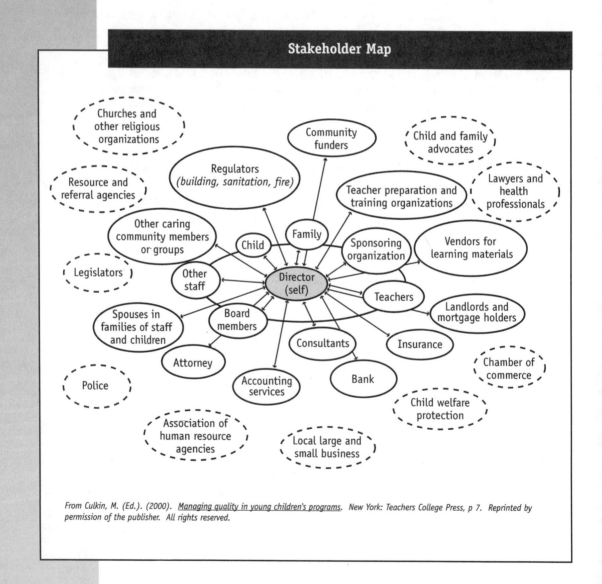

## Stakeholder Map

From Culkin, M. (Ed.). (2000). *Managing quality in young children's programs*. New York: Teachers College Press, p 7. *Reprinted by permission of the publisher. All rights reserved.*

The trend toward blended funding streams, coordinated delivery systems, community-based planning, collaborative data collection, service delivery networks, and other systemic changes has created demands on early childhood administrators for knowledge and skills not previously needed. Leaders must now have a broad and more sophisticated repertoire of communication skills, decision-making and problem-solving skills, interpersonal skills, and organizational skills to help them build alliances, negotiate differences, and pursue innovative strategies to enhance their program's viability. This means changes in the way early childhood directors spend their time—more public speaking, advocacy, grant writing, marketing, consensus building, and contacts with the media than ever before.

The bottom line is that high-quality early childhood programs are inextricably linked to the actions of their leaders. The complex nature of our field calls for a new kind of early childhood director—one who is interested in both the art and the science of leadership, willing to stretch, grow, and think in new ways.

My own research has confirmed that a director's level of formal and specialized training is a strong predictor of overall program quality, while years of directing a child care center are not as potent a predictor of quality. This is not to discount the importance of experience, but it is evident that directors need much more than a learning-along-the-way kind of knowledge to be successful. They need to make a serious commitment to their profession and to their personal and professional development in order to achieve the goal of administering an excellent program.

## The Good News—Leadership Ability Is Not Static

No matter where you start, you can get better. In my work training early childhood administrators, I have seen ordinary directors become extraordinary leaders. True, some people are born with natural gifts; but anecdotal evidence confirms that the ability to lead a center is really a collection of skills and dispositions, nearly all of which can be learned and nurtured.

Do you find yourself asking . . .

- how can I inspire and motivate others to pursue common goals?
- how do I make my values evident in my daily actions as a leader?
- how can I be a better role model for my staff?
- how do I craft a vision for my center when the future seems so uncertain?
- how can I build cohesive team spirit?

We have seen the last generation of center and nonprofit agency directors who will succeed in their jobs without substantive management education.

*David Renz*

11

- how do I handle difficult ethical dilemmas?
- how do I find the strength to make difficult decisions?
- how do I create a work climate that promotes and celebrates diversity?
- how do I encourage innovation and risk taking?
- how do I involve others in decisions and still maintain accountability?
- how can I help others find joy and fulfillment in their work?

If so, then *Leadership in Action* is for you. This book is not about formulas or quick solutions. It is about a way of thinking about your role and the vital work you do every day. Its chapters are filled with suggestions and examples from high-performing directors; however, the hard work only you can do. The transformation is from the inside out.

# CHAPTER 2

# Leadership as a Way of Thinking

While *Leadership in Action* stresses the importance of behavior—those things you do and say that support exemplary practices—your actions are only part of the story. Leadership begins in the head. It is a way of thinking about yourself and the vital role you play in your program.

In this chapter we'll grapple with the philosophical questions of what it means to be a leader and how you perceive yourself as a leader. We'll look at leadership as the exercise of influence, leadership as an expression of your values, and leadership as a statement of the hopes and dreams you have for yourself and your center. This discussion lays the foundation for addressing the behaviors and practices that you'll learn in later chapters.

## Leadership as the Exercise of Influence

Most early childhood directors readily accept the notion that an essential part of leadership is the ability to inspire, motivate, and affect the feelings and actions of others. But when the conversation expands to include a discussion of authority and the exercise of power, many in our ranks feel uncomfortable, believing these terms have negative connotations. This is unfortunate because how leaders view the authority and power relationships inherent in their organizations has everything to do with their ability to achieve their programs' missions.

Our beliefs about authority and power guide our behavior every day. Different organizational decisions—such as determining job titles, pay, and compensation levels; reporting relationships; providing access to information; and involving others in decision making—all relate to how you view authority and power. The equation does not include just you and your staff—it also includes your relationship with the children in your program, their families, the board, the center's neighbors, and the broader professional community in which you operate.

Authority and power are concepts early childhood directors can't ignore. Being clear about your own management philosophy as it relates to these issues will help you understand the subtleties between terms like *authoritarian* and *authoritative*, *cooperation* and *collaboration*, and *patronizing* and *empowering*. Put simply, how you view yourself as the person in charge impacts the interpersonal dynamics every day in your center in small and big ways.

**Sources of power.** Power is a dynamic that exists in all adult/child and adult/adult relationships. It is the ability to get others to do what you want them to do. In its simplest form we can think of power as control, authority, or dominance *over* another individual or as sharing authority and responsibility *with* another person. So the central question is not "Will power be used?" but rather "How can power be used wisely?" How can it be used to engage, guide, and support children, staff, and parents in the pursuit of common goals?

The concept of power can be further understood by exploring the reasons that prompt individuals to comply with requests, requirements, or demands from others. Early childhood directors derive power from personal as well as organizational sources. The table on page 15 summarizes five kinds of power that are at play in all types organizations, including early care and education programs. These five types of power can be grouped into two broad categories— organizational and personal.

Reward, coercive, and legitimate power are bound to the position in the organization. So the greater the authority attached to a position, the greater the potential for use of these types of power. In contrast, expert and referent power depend more on the personal attributes of the individual, such as personality, leadership style, knowledge, integrity, and interpersonal behavior. These types of power do not depend on occupying a formal position.

As you reflect on the use of different types of power in your program, consider the outcomes of each approach as they relate to your employees' behavior. Think of their behavior as falling on a continuum with resistance at one end, compliance in the middle, and commitment at the other end.

**resistance** ———→ ——→ — **compliance** ———→ ——→ — **commitment**

The use of reward power, so commonplace in organizations, promotes compliance with specific rules or requests. Over time, however, employees may perceive reward power as manipulative. When misused, reward power can result in competition among staff, thus undermining your efforts to establish norms of collaboration. Although coercive power yields short-term compliance, over time it results in resentment and alienation of staff. Teachers who quit without notice or walk off with a year's supply of colored markers are often retaliating in response to coercive power.

## Different Kinds of Power

### Organizational

- **Reward power** is a director's ability to influence staff by rewarding desired behavior. To the extent that directors control teaching schedules, classroom assignments, and routine housekeeping duties, they have reward power over teachers. In many programs, teachers comply with a director's requests because they expect to be rewarded for compliance—the director has established a quid pro quo relationship. In some programs, reward power is openly promoted through bonus or merit performance systems.

- **Coercive power** is essentially the flip side of reward power. Directors have the ability to influence staff by punishing them for undesirable behavior. Punishment can be in the form of a reprimand, undesirable work assignments, closer supervision, or even termination. Punishment can also be viewed as the absence of rewards or resources.

- **Legitimate power** is an individual's ability to influence behavior simply because of the formal authority accorded to the position. In most organizations employees readily accept that individuals in certain positions on the organizational chart have the right to make decisions and issue directives and that employees have an obligation to comply. Authority exercised through legitimate power is often expressed as orders, commands, directives, or instructions.

### Personal

- **Expert power** is directors' ability to influence others because of their credentials and specialized knowledge and skill. Staff believe that the director possesses knowledge and skills they do not have, so they willingly follow the director's lead.

- **Referent power** is based on the staff's respect and admiration for the director. Staff identify with the director because of his or her personality and interpersonal skills. The director is perceived as a role model to be emulated, and staff comply with requests because they respect the values and principles the director stands for.

*Adapted from French, J., & Raven, B. (1959). The bases of social power. In D. Cartwright (Ed.), Social studies in power (pp. 150-67). Ann Arbor, MI: Institute for Social Research.*

Legitimate power, like reward power, promotes compliance, but it seldom motivates staff to long-term commitment to a program. Expert power can move employees beyond mere compliance to deeper levels of commitment if they perceive that the knowledge and skill of the director (or other authority figures in the center) are essential in promoting their well-being. Referent power is the type of power most likely to promote long-term commitment to a center, particularly if staff identify with and admire the values and principles of the director or other leaders in the center.

**From power to empowerment.** Power need not be thought of as a negative or constraining force in early childhood organizations. In fact, by being aware of the power dynamics at play in programs, directors can become more cognizant of how they might put power to good use to energize and empower children, staff, and families. This requires a paradigm shift from thinking about power *over* others to think about power *with* others. The questions to ask yourself now are framed a bit differently:

- How can I help people feel more powerful?
- How can I turn the power pyramid upside down and use the influence and resources of my position to ignite passion and purpose in my staff?

Empowerment is the process through which directors share their legitimate authority and power, helping others use it in constructive ways to make decisions affecting themselves and their work. Empowerment happens when staff are helped to find greater meaning in their work, to meet higher level needs through their work, and to develop enhanced personal and professional capacities. This form of power is unlimited.

Like many leadership constructs, empowerment is best conceptualized on a continuum, with tight controls over all aspects of the center's operations at one end and complete delegation of authority and power at the other end. Most directors strive for a comfortable balance midway on the continuum, looking for ways to create more meaningful partnerships with both staff and parents about the issues that deeply affect their wellbeing but not abdicating oversight or accountability. The book *Circle of Influence: Implementing Shared Decision Making and Participative Management*, another volume in the Director's Toolbox Management Series, is a great resource for concrete suggestions on how to empower staff.

Letting go of the need to control is the first step to empowerment. It means viewing one's position as leader as that of a facilitator of growth and change—being accountable for the well-being of the larger organization by operating in the service of others rather than controlling them.

**A new model—facilitative leadership.** Rethinking personal conceptions of power and moving to a model of facilitative leadership means rethinking the specifics of how you can create partnerships in every facet of the center's operations. It means finding ways to give a greater voice to the staff on issues that affect them every day—allocation of educational resources, curriculum, scheduling. And it means constructing meaningful partnerships with families by providing them with a greater voice in their children's daily experiences and parent policies.

Directors who view themselves as facilitative leaders think about ways they can help individuals and groups in the center reflect on and improve the processes they use to solve problems and make decisions. In other words, facilitative leaders help others learn how to learn. They understand that while rewards and external controls generate compliance, it is staff's internal sense of mastery, accomplishment, and validation that generate their long-term commitment to a center.

Rather than nurturing staff reliance on expert or referent power, facilitative leaders seek to decrease the group's dependence on them as the leader by elevating expertise within the whole group and developing a sense of shared responsibility for both organizational problems and organizational achievements. A facilitative leader's influence does not stem from the authority of the position, but rather from his or her ability to help others accomplish what they want to accomplish.

Facilitative leadership is a reciprocal process between those who aspire to lead and those who choose to follow. It is not something that is done *to* people, but rather working *with* and *through* other people to achieve organizational goals. Trust is essential for this kind of leadership. Staff need to believe that you, the director, are operating in their best interest, not out of self-interest. Facilitative leaders exemplify the qualities of competence, connection, and character. They understand that leadership is not about being in charge, but about serving and supporting others. It is about compassion and the day-to-day practice of social justice in a caring community.

When the best leader's work is done, the people say, we did it ourselves.

*Lao-tzu*

## Moving to a Model of Facilitative Leadership

| Organizational component | Traditional leader | Facilitative leader |
|---|---|---|
| Information sharing | Director controls access to and flow of information pertaining to centerwide issues. | Information is shared broadly. Staff feel they are well informed about centerwide issues. |
| Problem solving | Director solves problems that staff present. | Director ensures that staff have access to relevant information to solve problems and intervenes only when necessary. |
| Decision making | Director either makes decisions alone or in consultation with staff. | Director supports multiple decision-making approaches, including consultative, collaborative, and delegated decision making, depending on the situation. |
| Conflict management | Director manages conflicts among employees. | Director helps employees learn how to manage their own conflicts and intervenes only when necessary. |
| Parent communications | Director is largely responsible for communicating and solving problems with parents. | Director works with staff to develop expectations and guidelines for communicating and problem solving with parents. |
| Community relations | Director serves as primary representative of the center in the community. | Director involves staff and parents in representing the center at different community functions. |
| Goal setting | Director writes organizational mission and sets goals for the center. | At least annually, the director, staff, and parents review the center's mission and establish new goals. |
| Group norms and culture | Director attempts to establish norms and influence the group culture implicitly. | Director and staff regularly discuss core values, principles, and ground rules as the basis for group norms and the center's culture. |
| Allocation of time | Director makes decisions about daily schedules, staffing plans, and scheduling of events. | Director and staff meet regularly to talk about daily schedules, staffing patterns, and scheduling of tasks that need to be done. |
| Recruiting and hiring staff | Director oversees the recruitment process and makes all hiring decisions. | Staff are involved in the recruiting, screening, and hiring of all new employees. |
| Job assignments | Director defines employees' roles and writes all job descriptions. | Director involves staff in updating their job descriptions on an annual basis. |
| Supervision and professional development | Director assumes primary responsibility for supervision and sets professional development goals for employees. | Director involves others (e.g., mentors, peer coaches) in the supervision process.  An individualized model of staff development is used in which staff and director together target annual professional development goals. |

| Organizational component | Traditional leader | Facilitative leader |
|---|---|---|
| Performance appraisal | Director assumes sole responsibility for performance appraisal. | A 360° feedback approach is used in which employees receive feedback on performance from the director, peers, and parents. |
| Compensation | Director determines pay and benefits for employees on a case-by-case basis. | A salary scale with clear criteria for promotion to the next level is reviewed with staff on an annual basis. Staff are involved in revising criteria as needed. |
| Physical environment | Director determines the physical layout of space and materials. | Director and staff together determine best use of space and materials. |
| Training | Director makes decisions about allocation of resources for training and the topics for staff development. | Director and staff together assess individual and group staff development needs and make decisions about allocation of resources for training. |
| Program evaluation | Director administers annual evaluation to elicit feedback from parents about the program. | Director elicits feedback about the program from parents, staff, and community members on an annual basis and shares the results of the evaluation with all stakeholders. |

Adapted from Schwarz, R. (2002). *The skilled facilitator: A comprehensive resource for consultants, facilitators, managers, trainers, and coaches.* San Francisco: Jossey-Bass.

## Leadership as an Expression of Your Values

If you think of some the great leaders who have inspired us through the ages— Jesus, Mahatma Gandhi, Abraham Lincoln, Pope John XXIII, Albert Schweitzer, Mother Teresa—their accomplishments tell only part of the story of why biographers write volumes about their lives. It is the values, beliefs, and deeply held principles made evident through their actions that define their characters and make them legends across time.

A value is a deeply held and enduring view of what we believe to be important and worthwhile. Our personal values shape our beliefs about what is important to pursue, how we treat others, and how we choose to spend our time. A belief is different from a value. It is our personal conviction that certain things are true or that certain statements are facts.

Complete these phrases with the first things that come to mind:

- I value ...
- I stand for ...
- I believe that ...
- I feel passionate about ...

Your responses no doubt capture just a few of the values, beliefs, and deeply held principles that make you a unique thinking, feeling, and acting human being from everyone else on the planet. You are, in essence, a complex combination of values and beliefs; some are immutable and strongly define your personality, some only slightly define who you are as an individual.

Mastering the technical skills of administration is not enough to become a respected leader of an early care and education program. The values and beliefs that give life to a director's convictions and are lived through daily actions are what distinguish ordinary from extraordinary directors. To effectively model the behavior they expect of others, early childhood leaders must be clear about their own values and belief systems.

**Personal values and beliefs.** Our core values cut across all aspects of our lives. They serve as a point of reference, a kind of moral compass for making daily decisions. They give rise to our fundamental commitments, the things in life that we consider worthy for their own sake. Because values influence and guide people's choices, being crystal clear about the beliefs and values that shape their identity is central for leaders in any setting. The values listed in the table on page 21 are those frequently cited by people as being important.

While values certainly reflect our family upbringing and cultural backgrounds, they are also shaped by personal experiences, education, and societal influences. You can think of your values as the lenses in a pair of glasses. They bring focus and clarity to your interpretation of the world and are strong motivators for personal action.

What does this mean in your day-to-day life as a director? If you value cooperation, for example, you probably spend a lot of time encouraging staff to share resources and work together on team assignments. If you value independence, you may structure work assignments to promote autonomy and personal achievement instead of team efforts. If you value neatness, you probably praise staff for their tidy and organized classrooms. If you value creativity, however, you may be more tolerant of the mess that often accompanies inspiration and imagination. We all value different things and can't presume that others think or feel as we do.

## Some Things People Value

| | | |
|---|---|---|
| Accountability | Family | Positive attitude |
| Achievement | Fairness | Power |
| Adventure | Forgiveness | Prestige |
| Aesthetics | Freedom | Privacy |
| Affiliation | Friendship | Recognition |
| Altruism | Happiness | Reliability |
| Beauty | Harmony | Responsibility |
| Challenge | Honesty | Security |
| Change | Independence | Self-control |
| Collaboration | Innovation | Self-expression |
| Community | Intellectual stimulation | Self-respect |
| Compensation | Intimacy | Service |
| Competence | Integrity | Social justice |
| Competition | Justice | Social relationships |
| Cooperation | Knowledge | Spiritual growth |
| Creativity | Learning | Stability |
| Decisiveness | Logic | Teamwork |
| Democracy | Loyalty | Tolerance |
| Diversity | Mutual respect | Tradition |
| Efficiency | Nature | Tranquility |
| Equity | Neatness | Trust |
| Environment | Open communication | Variety |
| Excellence | Perseverance | Wealth |
| Excitement | Personal growth | Wisdom |

Even with commonly identified values such as honesty, responsibility, caring, happiness, self-respect, and harmony, there may be little agreement on what behaviors and actions give evidence to these values. That is because every person represents a rich composite of values, each influencing decisions and actions in slightly different ways.

*Constance is the director of a child care program that is part of a United Way agency. Her center serves 120 families with low-incomes. She oversees a staff of fourteen. Constance was pleased that the agency's human resources department decided to include a values clarification activity at its annual retreat because she hoped it would give her insight into how to deal with a few of her teachers whom she describes as "operating on a different wavelength."*

*During the exercise, individuals were asked to share one or two of their core values and some examples of how they believed they put their values into action. Constance was surprised to see that both she and José, the lead teacher in her school-age program, selected mutual respect and responsibility as two of their most cherished values. She was surprised, because José was one of the teachers with whom she had been having some difficulty in interpersonal relations. While he was a terrific teacher with the school-age kids and the parents adored him, Constance felt he just didn't live up to her performance expectations. He was often late to staff meetings and needed frequent reminders to turn in required paperwork.*

*As part of the group discussion when staff shared examples of how they put their values into action, Constance indicated that "being on time" and "following through on commitments" was how she judged herself and others in regard to mutual respect and responsibility. She was surprised to hear that José, while embracing the same values, interpreted them quite differently as his personal code for conduct. Mutual respect to José meant "never interrupting anyone while they were talking, always deferring to authority, and listening to others with focused attention." Responsibility meant "giving 100% in energy and commitment to the children and making sure they were always safe."*

*The discussion gave Constance an important insight into herself as a leader. She realized that she not only expected everyone to embrace her values but also her idiosyncratic interpretation of her values.*

Take a few minutes now to complete Exercise 1. This exercise is designed to help you understand the values that are most important to you and clarify the nuances of how you define and live these values in your daily life.

From the table on page 21, select the ten values that are most important to you. Feel free to add values that are important but are missing from this list. Next to each value, write your definition of what this value means to you or an example of a behavior that demonstrates how you live this value in your personal or professional life.

| Value | Definition or Behavior |
| --- | --- |
| 1. _____ | _____ |
| 2. _____ | _____ |
| 3. _____ | _____ |
| 4. _____ | _____ |
| 5. _____ | _____ |
| 6. _____ | _____ |
| 7. _____ | _____ |
| 8. _____ | _____ |
| 9. _____ | _____ |
| 10. _____ | _____ |

From the list of ten important values you have created, put a star next to the four or five values that are *most important* in shaping your beliefs, attitudes, and behavior. Reflect on the importance of these core values as a cluster. How do they work together to help shape your belief system and guide your actions?

**Does your rhetoric match your actions?** On a personal level, the importance of exploring values lies in seeing if your rhetoric matches your actions. How directors spend their time is the single clearest indicator to others about what's important to them. If a director says that her top priority is her relationship with parents, and yet her office door is closed during arrival and dismissal, there may be a disconnect between espoused values and action.

Conducting a personal audit of how you allocate your time, how you spend your money, and where you focus your attention provides clear evidence of how your espoused values do or don't match your behavior. The car you drive, the clothes you wear, the food you eat, the things that make you laugh, and other personal idiosyncrasies all communicate your personal values.

One director decorates her office walls with the children's artwork; another displays photographs of his family; still another displays her professional degrees and certificates. These decisions send signals to others about what a director sees as important. Even the layout and design of space in a center—the size of the director's office, the presence of a parent lounge, the availability of a professional library for staff—reverberate with values.

The form and substance of written communications, as well, convey personal values. Even the appearance of memos and newsletters—the attention to detail, the information included, and the use or absence of educational jargon—provides evidence of values. There's no avoiding it. Everything you do or say communicates something about you and the values you embrace.

**Organizational values and beliefs.** The most valuable conversations we have in our programs are conversations that reveal our core values. As the vignette about Constance and José so perfectly illustrates, the same value can mean different things to different people. These individual interpretations lived through our actions every day can give rise to misunderstanding, even conflict, in our work settings.

Your role as a leader is to help staff clarify their own core values and then together develop a set of shared values that define excellence and success for your program. This is not an easy task. It is also not something that is accomplished in a single, hour-long staff meeting or one-day retreat. It is an ongoing process that takes place over months, even years. Engaging your staff in a dialogue about values will help you understand the motivations for people's behavior and help you shape the essential values that define your program. In the process, you and your staff will wrestle with these fundamental questions:

- What do we stand for?
- What behaviors provide concrete evidence of our shared values?
- How do we treat the children in our care?
- How do we treat their parents?
- How do we interact as a group of adults working side by side every day?
- How do we define success in our program?
- How do we want to be seen by the community?

If you look at the most successful companies in America, you'll note that they are built on a clear and shared understanding of the company's core values. The Walt Disney Company provides a perfect example of how a company's values translate into action. The four values of the Disney resorts and theme parks—safety, courtesy, the show (being in character), and efficiency—are introduced to employees during the hiring process and are reinforced at virtually every company meeting during the year. For any Disney employee there is simply no misunderstanding what those four core values mean in expected behavior every day on the job.

One example of how Disney puts these values into action is called Take Five. Every day employees (called *cast members*) are encouraged to take five minutes to do something special for a guest. The company calls it being aggressively friendly. Cast members look for opportunities to do little things for guests that create a magical memory associated with their visit. For example, when the housekeeper in one of the resort hotels learned that a guest was not feeling well, she took the personal initiative to bring her a bowl of chicken soup from the resort restaurant.

Your center may never become as well known as a Disney resort, but the values you establish with your staff can create magical moments just as powerful for the children and families you serve. Here is an example of a value statement developed by the staff of a part-day preschool program.

## Highland Hills Preschool

### *We value ...*

- **a curriculum that emerges** from the needs and interests of children and teachers.
- **parents as partners** in documenting children's learning.
- **diversity** in cultural background, learning styles, and expressed opinions.
- **a sense of community** in the classroom, in the staff room, and in our neighborhood.
- **active participation** of staff and parents in centerwide decisions.
- **continuity and stability** in relationships between children and their teachers.
- **openness and directness** in interpersonal relations at every level of the organization.
- **respect for the environment** inside and outside the classroom.

So how do you open the discussion about individual and shared values at your center? Appendix A is a Beliefs and Values Questionnaire you can use to get the ball rolling. This is a terrific resource because it focuses on the beliefs and values teachers have about their educational and caregiving roles. Focusing on personal values about children and families and the educational outcomes of your center is a powerful way to stimulate the broader discussion about other organizational values.

Centerwide discussions about values should help your staff explore the degree to which they live their values. In other words, are the value statements staff espouse just empty platitudes, or do staff genuinely feel they live and breathe their values in their daily interactions with one another? That's why it is not enough to simply make a list of core values. It's the definition and examples that give life to our values and make them understood by all.

**Reinforcing values through the questions you ask and the stories you tell.**
The best way to reinforce a center's core values is to consciously think about them as a framework for structuring interpersonal actions. This means every time you write a memo to your staff, respond to an e-mail, send a thank you, or leave a voice mail message for someone, you should think of it as an opportunity to reinforce one of your center's core values. "Jamie, thanks for helping Blanca with her computer yesterday. It's that kind of cooperative spirit that makes this center a great place to work." "Malcolm, it took courage to make the comment you made at our staff meeting yesterday. I really valued your openness and directness in communication."

Think also of the important questions that correspond to each of your center's core values. Every opportunity you have, ask these questions. This helps others to be more conscious about what they are doing to put the center's values into practice. For example, if one of your program's core values is *personal growth*, you can ask, "How will this decision help promote the personal growth of our staff?" If one of your core values is *community*, ask "How will this action reinforce our goal of promoting a sense of community?"

Another sure-fire way to reinforce the center's core values is to regularly share stories about everyday experiences that capture the essence of those values. Vignettes told and retold to staff, parents, and other constituencies will help them understand what makes your program unique.

The director of Highland Hills Preschool, for example, loves to tell the story of how the teachers and children at the center began a community garden. The garden project was actually prompted by a comment made by one of the moms who regularly volunteered at the center. She had recently moved to a new house and lamented that her backyard was too shaded to plant a vegetable garden. The comment made the children and teachers think how they might use a plot of sunny playground space for an environmental awareness project. One idea led to another, and before long the neighborhood had a full-fledged community garden. This story told regularly by the director to visitors of the center demonstrates two of the center's cherished core values—a sense of community and respect for the environment.

## Leadership as a Statement of Your Hopes and Dreams

Rare is the director who doesn't feel caught in a whirlwind of activity created by the daily demands of the administrative role. Menus to review, children to console, prospective parents to enroll—the nitty-gritty of the director's job leaves precious little time to stand back and envision the future.

It's no wonder when directors are interviewed about their goals for their programs, their aspirations seem flat—so concrete, so limited, so narrow in scope. A new roof, a new climbing structure for the playground, new cots, and a fresh coat of paint for the toddler room. "I've never dared to think big," confesses Candace, the director of a large for-profit program in an urban setting. "I guess being fully staffed and fully enrolled would be my measure of success." Candace is cautiously optimistic about the chances of achieving her goal. Other directors who are less sanguine measure success as simply the absence of crises in their programs.

Directors who dare to dream big, who have a compelling sense of purpose and vision for their programs, are indeed rare in our profession. This is understandable. For many, the gravitational forces of limited resources, demands for accountability, and an inhospitable regulatory environment are just too strong to overcome.

But how is it that some early childhood directors seem undaunted by the limiting realities of the early childhood field? Despite the same obstacles, they create organizations that achieve extraordinary outcomes for children and families. The key to their success is their ability to breathe life into their hopes and dreams and help others envision the exciting possibilities the future holds. These directors see themselves as agents of change whose calling is to forge a unity of purpose that creates the will and the momentum for achieving their vision.

**Connecting the dots...values...mission...vision.** Helen Keller was once asked if there was anything worse than living without sight. She replied, "Living without vision." Wise words indeed from a woman whose achievements astounded the world. A vision is like a lighthouse, a point in the distance that gives direction through the fog. It is not something that happens by accident; it is created purposefully. Creating a vision is about creating an organization that expresses your deepest values about children, family, work, achievement, community, and society. It comes from the heart. In essence, it is your scenario for a preferred future.

As director your greatest challenge is to let your vision, not your current resources, drive your decision-making process.

*Margie Carter and Deb Curtis*

A vision is different from a mission statement. A mission statement is more intellectual; it comes from the head. Mission statements describe the purpose of an organization and answer the question, why do we exist? An early childhood program achieves its mission by accomplishing various goals, which in turn are achieved by performing various tasks. A clearly articulated mission statement serves as a kind of yardstick with which to measure and evaluate an organization's activities.

The problem with most mission statements is that they are simply too long. A good mission statement should be no more than one or two sentences. It should be easily understood and simple to memorize and repeat. The core elements of a mission statement for early childhood programs are often very similar and include phrases like "We provide care and education for young children to help them achieve success in school, become productive future citizens, and develop into life-long learners." These noble sentiments are important, but they say nothing about what distinguishes one center from another. There is so much more that centers can be reaching for. It is the vision statement that takes an organization's values and mission to a higher level.

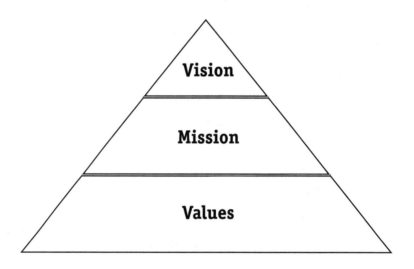

While a mission statement focuses on the purpose of your program, a *vision statement* is a mental picture of what you hope to accomplish—it is the end result you will achieve if your mission is carried out. A vision statement should be filled with descriptive details that breathe life into your dreams but are still anchored in reality. Together your mission and vision statements can serve as a template for initiating new programs, monitoring activities, and evaluating progress in your organization.

**Getting started.** Developing a vision statement doesn't require special prescient talents or gazing into a crystal ball, but it does require a commitment of time to reflect on the deeper purposes behind your center's mission and the legacy for which you want to be remembered. Take a moment now to complete Exercise 2. This exercise will get the creative juices flowing by helping you clarify your ideal.

What would you like to hear when people describe your program? Write a dozen or so words or phrases that describe your ideal program.

_____     _____

_____     _____

_____     _____

_____     _____

_____     _____

_____     _____

_____     _____

What are some of the things you'd like more of in your program?

_____     _____

_____     _____

What are some of the things you'd like less of in your program?

_____     _____

_____     _____

N ot much happens without a dream. And for something great to happen, there must be a great dream.

*Robert Greenleaf*

29

Developing a vision statement for your program is not a solitary exercise. No matter how capable you think you are, you can't do it alone. The essence of vision building is engaging in meaningful discussions with the people who are at the heart of your enterprise—teachers, board members, parents, and community representatives. Here are some questions to get you started:

- What would a program look like if it succeeded every day in creating memorable childhood experiences full of joy and laughter, adventure, and a sense of wonder?
- What does it mean to be engaged in meaningful work that makes a difference in the world?
- What would it feel like to be part of an organization where loyalty and commitment go hand in hand with high expectations and peak performance?
- What does it mean to be part of a learning community where children, staff, and parents grow together?
- What would it take to build a strong community that promotes access, equity, and social justice?

Involving the people who will be living the vision has the ancillary benefit of strengthening the very relationships that will help ensure that the vision becomes reality. Crafting a vision statement can be an empowering process that unites individuals in a common cause. When people feel like their voices have been heard and their ideas taken seriously, their commitment to the program rises commensurately.

**Going public.** Creating a compelling vision statement is only the first step to making it a reality. At some point you need to go public with your ideas, sharing them with a broader audience. This doesn't mean that you need the charismatic appeal of a Martin Luther King Jr. delivering his inspirational "I Have a Dream" speech, but you do need to be credible, persuasive, and genuine in the eyes of those you lead.

The most important aspect of your leadership role is communicating your organization's vision in a way that connects with, and gives clear direction to, those in it. Communicating your vision for the future means helping people make the quantum leap from expecting the ordinary to anticipating the extraordinary.

Take some time to think carefully about how you "package" your vision so you can communicate your ideas to your constituents clearly and succinctly. Your vision should include the major accomplishments you will attain as an organization, the level of quality you will achieve, and the character of the relationships you will have with children, their families, and the community.

People buy into the leader, then the vision.

*John Maxwell*

30

The key is to distill these ideas into images, symbols, or metaphors that best represent your vision of the future. Used repeatedly, these mental pictures will help shape people's expectations of you and your program. They'll begin to see what you want them to see, the essence of your vision unfolding. They'll have a vision mind-set.

While visionary pronouncements are important, don't forget that words are not enough to make your vision take hold. The real work takes place every day at your center. In your leadership role, your job is to help each person on your team understand unequivocally what it means to support your center's vision. Employees need to know how the vision relates to them directly, how their daily actions are part of a greater whole moving the program forward toward a more preferred ideal. Only in this way will your vision unite, inspire, and give purpose.

What you leave behind is not what is engraved in stone monuments, but what is woven into the lives of others.

*Pericles*

# CHAPTER 3

# The Starting Point—
# Know Thyself

Socrates was right!   You can't lead others unless you
first understand yourself.  The quest for leadership must
begin with an inner quest to discover who you are—
your passions, values, talents, personal resources, and
even those foibles and annoying habits you might
prefer not to acknowledge.  The insight that comes
from self-awareness will help you appreciate the unique
gifts you have to offer your organization and the
importance of surrounding yourself with others who
complement (and not necessarily compliment) your unique skill set and
personality.  Self-awareness generates self-confidence—a faith in your own ability
to meet the challenges of leadership and work with others to achieve your vision.

Objective introspection gives you insight into your emotions, an essential
ingredient in effective leadership.  When you can recognize and manage your
own emotions, you are better equipped to understand the emotions of others.
Self-aware leaders are attuned to their emotional reflexes and understand how
their behavior affects the job performance of others.  If you are aware, then you
are better able to adapt your style as needed to accommodate the demands of
different situations.

Self-awareness also means having a clear picture of your internal motives, those
things that drive you to say what you say and do what you do.  Peeling away
the layers of your motivations is not always a comfortable process, but it is a
necessary step if your goal is to become an authentic leader known for personal
integrity.  In Chapter 6 we'll talk more about what it means to "walk the talk."

Think of the insights that come from self-awareness as the ultimate navigation
system to maximize your personal performance.  The first step in the process is
to take a thorough and candid inventory of your strengths and weaknesses as
well as your physical, intellectual, social, and emotional resources.  This is not
a one-time endeavor; rather it is a continuous process that involves ongoing
personal reflection as well as soliciting feedback from others.  In this chapter
we'll only scratch the surface of this important topic.

Before we launch into a discussion of these important issues, however, let's first
take a look at the leaders, mentors, and role models in your life who have
inspired you and helped shape your thoughts, ideals, purposes, and passions.

## Which Leaders Have Inspired You or Disappointed You?

In her book *Lanterns: A Memoir of Mentors,* Marion Wright Edelman stresses that most people are influenced by several mentors during the course of their lives, not just one or two people. Sometimes it is a well-known person you've come to know through the front pages of the newspaper. Most often, though, it is a person close to you—a relative, teacher, friend, or supervisor—who has inspired you to be your best. Think about the influential leaders and mentors in your life as you take a moment to complete Exercise 3.

### exercise 3

Write the names of two or three people whom you respect and admire for their leadership abilities. Think of people who have inspired or mentored you to be your best; people who made you say "Wow, I wish I could be like ..." Next to their names, write the two or three traits or personal characteristics that set these individuals apart from others. Then in the adjacent space, add a specific example or two of how they put that quality into practice. Be as detailed as possible in describing their behavior.

| Person | Trait | Specific Behaviors |
|--------|-------|--------------------|
| _____ | _____ | _____ |
|        | _____ | _____ |
|        | _____ | _____ |
| _____ | _____ | _____ |
|        | _____ | _____ |
|        | _____ | _____ |
| _____ | _____ | _____ |
|        | _____ | _____ |
|        | _____ | _____ |

Now think about all the supervisors, bosses, and managers you've worked for as you complete this sentence.

*I do my most effective work for leaders who . . .*

_____

_____

Thinking about the traits, dispositions, skills, and specific behaviors that inspire you to peak performance can serve as a guide as you seek to expand your own repertoire of leadership skills and support the work of others.

There are many leadership lessons we can learn from individuals in other fields and disciplines. This is one of the reasons I love to read autobiographies and biographies. One of my favorites is *Personal History* by Katherine Graham. Mrs. Graham was thrust into a career in publishing and business with virtually no experience. She drew on her natural instincts, strength of character, and her personal charm to forge what today is one of the country's leading media and education businesses, The Washington Post Company. Along the way she stood her ground and took the heat on issues of principle. She surrounded herself with smart, capable people who shared her vision. And she encouraged those she hired to think for themselves and stand up for what they believe.

I loved this autobiography because although Katherine Graham was confident, her insecurities were deep and wide. "In truth," she confessed, "I didn't even know how much I didn't know, or the complexity of what lay before me. What I did know was that I wasn't at all sure that I could do what was going to be required of me."

Being overwhelmed by the scope and responsibility of a leadership position is certainly not a phenomenon experienced solely by Katherine Graham. Many famous figures in history write about being thrust into positions of awesome responsibility and feeling utterly overwhelmed. The experience is common enough that social psychologists refer to it as the *imposter syndrome*. You may have experienced such feelings yourself when you assumed your first job as a director. A key trait in strong leaders, however, is the capacity to meet the challenges of their new roles and find the fortitude and determination to triumph over their fears.

Sandra Day O'Connor, the first woman appointed to the Supreme Court, has also written a compelling memoir. She recounts the difficulty of getting her first job after graduating from Stanford Law School. She interviewed for a position and was told she would not be hired as a law associate but could consider a secretarial position at the firm if she wanted to. She had the confidence in herself to tell the attorney that she wasn't interested in the secretarial position but that she would work for the firm for a year without pay just to prove her worth as a lawyer. The rest, of course, is history.

Justice O'Connor's memoir is a reminder of how lonely being a trailblazer can be. She zeros in on the extraordinary pressure to perform that is put on leaders who are "firsts." It wasn't until Ruth Bader Ginsburg was appointed to the Court, Justice O'Connor says, that she could relax and feel like all eyes weren't focused on her.

While the lessons we learn from extraordinary leaders are helpful, we can also learn powerful lessons from the "unleaders" who have been part of our world of work. My guess is you've had a boss, supervisor, manager, or agency official who held a leadership position but did not live up to your expectations of how a leader should act. He may have been indecisive, unreliable, or inconsistent in his actions. Perhaps she showed favoritism or outright bias and discrimination in making decisions. Or he simply may have been in over his head regarding the demands of the job, incompetent but unaware of his own inadequacies.

The emotional scars and organizational turmoil that can result from ineffective, unethical, or just plain incompetent leadership can leave us disillusioned, frustrated, and angry. Seeing the damage done by poor leaders can serve as a powerful reminder of those behaviors and traits we never want to emulate.

## Which Traits Define Your Leadership Style?

Case studies of exemplary leaders from history and from your own experience provide ample evidence that there is no one best style of leadership. Leaders come in all shapes and sizes. Some have a bold, assertive style and enjoy the attention of being in the spotlight. Others transform organizations in less flamboyant and outspoken ways. How about you? Think about the traits and characteristics that define your leadership style as you complete Exercise 4.

**exercise 4**

Read through the list of traits in the accompanying table "Some Traits We Associate with Good Leaders" and select **five** traits that best capture the essence of your leadership style. If you think of a personal trait that isn't on the list, feel free to add it.

1. _____

2. _____

3. _____

4. _____

5. _____

Now go through the list again and select **three** more traits that you would like to develop over the next year.

1. _____

2. _____

3. _____

## Some Traits We Associate With Good Leaders

| | | |
|---|---|---|
| Accessible | Empathetic | Open |
| Achiever | Energetic | Optimistic |
| Acknowledges mistakes | Engaging | Organized |
| Ambitious | Enthusiastic | Passionate |
| Analytical | Ethical | Patient |
| Articulate | Fair | Playful |
| Assertive | Fast paced | Poised |
| Available | Flexible | Positive |
| Calm | Focused | Practical |
| Collaborative | Friendly | Precise |
| Compassionate | Generous | Predictable |
| Confident | Good listener | Problem solver |
| Conscientious | Gracious | Reliable |
| Considerate | Helpful | Resilient |
| Consistent | Honest | Responsible |
| Courageous | Humble | Resourceful |
| Creative | Humorous | Risk taker |
| Decisive | Inquisitive | Social |
| Dependable | Inspiring | Strategic |
| Determined | Intelligent | Supportive |
| Direct | Introspective | Tactful |
| Disciplined | Knowledgeable | Trustworthy |
| Dynamic | Objective | Visionary |

An important point to keep in mind as you pinpoint the traits that define your unique leadership style is that sometimes the very traits that make you highly effective in one situation may actually undermine your effectiveness in another situation. Look back at the five traits in Exercise 4 that you selected to best define your leadership style. Are there any that work better in some situations than in others? Self-knowledge about how your defining traits can support but also limit you from achieving desired outcomes allows you to flex your style, modifying and adjusting your signature themes as the situation demands.

## How Effective Do You Feel in Your Leadership Role?

Your gut feeling about how you handle the day-in, day-out demands of your job can serve as a pretty accurate barometer of how effective you actually are in your leadership role. Here are some questions that will lead to the heart of your perception of your own leadership effectiveness:

- Do you always feel like you're swamped, fighting fires, barely meeting deadlines, and living on the edge till the next crisis?
- Are you burdened with more paperwork than you had a year ago?
- Do you find people seeking your permission to carry out tasks they should be assuming on their own?
- Do you receive a lot of work-related telephone calls at home in the evening or on weekends?
- Do you feel you can give honest feedback to members of your staff without their getting defensive?
- Do you find yourself spending more time working on small details than on planning and visioning for the future?
- Do you need to repeat directions and suggestions over and over before they are followed?
- Does the conversation stop or change focus when you walk into a room full of teachers?
- Do you feel that you have to remind others in subtle ways how hard you work because they don't seem to appreciate how much you do?

If you answered yes to five or more of these questions, you probably feel a bit dispirited and overwhelmed by the scope of your responsibilities. You may even be questioning whether the job is really the right fit for you. Don't give up hope. Many of the concerns in this list relate to time and task management issues that are easily improved with focused determination. Others relate more to your leadership style and the interpersonal behaviors you exhibit.

Certainly there is no easy formula for learning effective leadership skills. The principles of good management must be personalized to fit your individual style and the unique set of circumstances in which you work. The good news is that effective leadership can be studied, practiced, and refined. In the process you can attain that all-important balance: achieving organizational success while still meeting your own needs.

## What Image Do You Project?

You've heard it before—first impressions are lasting impressions. Ask yourself, do I project a professional image? Think about the way you dress, your overall grooming, making eye contact, body posture, and even the energy you communicate in your handshake. The way you choose to present yourself can have a profound effect on how seriously you are taken.

Essential to effective leadership is effective speaking. The ability to communicate persuasively lies at the core of leadership, whether your goal is to convince one person in a private meeting or sway an entire organization. Have you taken time to really listen to your voice recently? If not, audiotape yourself at a meeting and play it back. Is your voice dull or vibrant? Do you exude confidence, or does your speech pattern include hesitations such as "ah," "you know," "um," and "uh"? Does the pitch of your voice rise at the end of sentences, creating a string of declarative statements that sound more like questions?

Most people focus far more on what they want to say than on how they deliver their message. But pitch, volume, and diction are all aspects of voice control that affect how seriously you are taken. It is possible to train your voice to be clear, strong, and decisive. When she was First Lady, Eleanor Roosevelt took elocution lessons to improve her presence. She ultimately wound up as representative to the United Nations, where her voice was heard around the world.

While voice control takes effort, there is one aspect of speaking that is easier to correct. It has to do with how much you say. When it comes to speaking, more is often less. A constant stream of words flowing from your mouth can reduce your credibility. It takes discipline to keep your words few but full. Try to become known as a person who has something to say when you speak. This means reducing the use of jargon as much as possible and avoiding the trap of repeating yourself over and over to make your point.

S pread the message wherever you go and speak only if you need to.

*St. Francis of Assisie*

## What Are Your Assumptions About People?

Examining your assumptions about people can be a valuable aid to understanding leadership behavior. Take a few minutes to complete Exercise 5 before reading the rest of this section.

Below are six pairs of statements. In each pair, check (✓) the one statement that better represents your beliefs about people and the work they do in your organization. When you have completed the exercise, you should have six items checked.

1. ❑ It is only natural for teachers to do as little work as they can get away with.

2. ❑ When teachers avoid work, it is usually because their job is deprived of meaning.

3. ❑ If teachers have access to information about centerwide issues, their commitment to the center will be increased.

4. ❑ If teachers have access to more information than they need to do their specific job, they will most likely misuse it.

5. ❑ One problem with asking for ideas from teachers is that their perspective is too limited for their suggestions to have much practical value.

6. ❑ Asking teachers for their ideas broadens their perspective and results in generating more useful suggestions.

7. ❑ If teachers are allowed to set their own performance goals, they would likely set them lower than a director would.

8. ❑ If teachers are allowed to set their own performance goals, they would probably set them higher than a director would.

9. ❑ People will work harder if they are accountable for their own behavior and correcting their own mistakes.

10. ❑ People tend to lower their standards if they are not supervised carefully and corrected for their mistakes.

11. ❑ If you pay employees more, they will be less concerned with intangibles like recognition and acknowledgement of a job well done.

12. ❑ If you give employees interesting and challenging work, they are less likely to complain about their pay and compensation.

Directors' assumptions about their employees relate to their beliefs about human nature and how best to motivate people to high levels of performance. An assumption is an opinion that something is true. Your assumptions about people will determine how you treat them. That is because what we assume about people is what we look for. And what we look for is what we usually find.

The work of Douglas McGregor serves as a good starting point for understanding this aspect of our leadership behavior. McGregor postulates that there are essentially two ways that leaders view employees in the work setting. Theory X holds that people dislike working and that they will avoid it at all costs if they can. This view is based on the belief that individuals want to avoid challenge and responsibility; what people really want most is job security. Directors who ascribe to Theory X assumptions tend to see their role as one of controlling, directing, coercing, and prodding individuals to do what they should. They use supervision, time clocks, and a range of other external controls and rewards to keep people in line.

Theory Y assumptions contend that work is intrinsically rewarding for people, a natural extension of their identity. This view is based on the belief that individuals work toward things to which they are committed, and this commitment is the basis of job satisfaction. Under the right conditions, people will not only accept responsibility but will seek it.

Subscribing to this set of assumptions means that a leader has faith in employees to structure their own goals and that individuals are their own best source of motivation. If their work is properly structured, employees will be motivated by the results of their efforts more than by external rewards or other controls. Theory Y leaders focus on the nature of relationships and creating a work environment that encourages commitment to personal and organizational objectives.

Theory X and Theory Y are clearly contrasting beliefs about human nature and the real-world conditions of work. Theory X views motivation as a carrot-and-stick set of transactions and promotes the necessity for close supervision of employees. Collaboration and participative management in this belief system are viewed as a nice ideal in the abstract but really not practical in the real world. Theory Y leadership is characterized by commitment to shared goals, high levels of trust, and authentic, open relationships.

Look back now at the answers you gave to Exercise 5. Theory X assumptions are associated with questions 1, 4, 5, 7, 10, 11. Think about how your assumptions are related to your expectations for the employees working at your center.

## What Is Your Work Orientation?

The effective early childhood administrator has the skills of both a task specialist and a human relations specialist. This means balancing the needs of the organization (budgets, maintenance, planning) to run efficiently while still meeting the needs of the people who work at the center (guidance, motivation, counseling, modeling). It is a rare person indeed who can juggle both sets of responsibilities and maintain their equilibrium. Many directors are more proficient in one set of skills than the other. Exercise 6 provides an opportunity for you to assess your preferences as they relate to your work orientation.

### exercise 6

For each set of paired statements, circle A or B next to the sentence that better describes your work orientation.

A. I prefer working alone
B. I prefer working with other people

A. I like to work on a single task at a time
B. I like to work on multiple tasks simultaneously

A. I am good at noticing details
B. I am good at seeing the big picture

A. I engage in conversation to share information
B. I engage in conversation to make connections

A. I need a sense of closure on projects
B. I don't mind leaving projects uncompleted

A. I approach my work in a systematic way
B. I approach my work in an unstructured way

A. I make decisions based on facts and logic
B. I make decisions based on intuition

A. I am regularly on time for appointments
B. I am frequently late for appointments

A. I think inside the box
B. I think outside the box

A. People view me as methodical and precise
B. People view me as flexible and carefree

A. I make decisions easily and quickly
B. I take my time making decisions

A. I focus on what people say
B. I focus on the feelings behind what people say

A. I work well with "to do" lists and deadlines
B. I do just fine without a "to do" list

A. I am more planned than spontaneous
B. I am more spontaneous than planned

A. I keep my feelings to myself
B. I freely show my feelings

A. I value clear and precise thinking
B. I value creative thinking

A. Other people's opinions matter only a little to me
B. Other people's opinions matter a great deal to me

A. I consider myself a paper person
B. I consider myself a people person

Tally the total number of As and Bs you circled. The A statements describe characteristics typical of a task-oriented work style. The B statements describe characteristics of a process-oriented work style.

Achieving center goals is most important in a *task-oriented* work style. Directors with this preference have a strong concern for high performance and accomplishing the business of the day. The emphasis here is on structuring the work, specifying the tasks to be performed, establishing channels of communication, and designating responsibilities. The focus is on planning, following procedures, and applying uniform standards and expectations for all. The needs of the center come first.

Many employees like task-oriented directors because job descriptions and policies are clearly defined, paychecks are never late, minutes are promptly sent out after meetings, and the supply cabinet is always stocked with paint and glue. The keys words for this work orientation are efficiency and productivity. The downside of this style is that some staff view the director as too structured, inflexible, and bureaucratic.

Achieving harmonious group relations is foremost in a *process-oriented* work style. Leaders with this preference have a strong concern for nurturing relationships, building mutual trust, and maintaining comfortable, friendly, and satisfying working conditions. Directors with this orientation ensure that everyone's point of view is heard, that due process is followed, and that congenial relationships are fostered. Feelings and emotions are valued as much as intellect and know-how.

Many employees like process-oriented directors because their hard work is validated and they are made to feel special. The key words for this work orientation are collaboration and collegiality. The downside of this style is that some staff may complain about the lack of order and coordination in the center.

Clearly the goal for effective leadership is to try to achieve a balance between these two orientations—an integrated style that gets the tasks done but also shows high regard for the process and the needs of people carrying out the work. This is easier said than done. The reason it is so difficult is that your employees have their own preferred work orientation. Those who are more task focused will appreciate the things you do to promote efficiency and get the work done: those who focus more on process will appreciate the things you do to create congenial relationships and honor each person's voice. Take a look at the table on the following page. Where do you stand in achieving a balance?

## Achieving a Balance

| Task Oriented | Process Oriented |
|---|---|
| Setting goals and objectives | Connecting and socializing with colleagues |
| Disseminating information | Hearing all perspectives |
| Making decisions | Attending to personal needs |
| Attending to details | Brainstorming |
| Following the agenda | Nurturing interpersonal understanding |
| Solving problems | Encouraging full discussion |
| Planning work | Attending to people's feelings |
| Watching the clock | Paraphrasing for validation |
| Learning new skills | Valuing creative thinking |
| Staying on task | Probing for understanding |
| Scheduling events | Respecting diverse opinions |
| Coming to closure | Providing recognition |

## What Are Your Self-Expectations?

Even if you don't know the difference between a Kenmore iron and a Ping iron, you can't help but be impressed by the world-class act of Annika Sorenstam in daring to be the first female to play in a PGA tour event since 1945. For many on the pro golf circuit, this media-hyped event became a battle of the sexes. Sports commentators delighted in asking male pro golfers if their egos would be bruised if Sorenstam out-birdied them on the first round of the tournament held at the Colonial Country Club. For Sorenstam, however, the issue wasn't men versus women; it was challenging herself to do her personal best. When asked how she found the strength and courage to challenge the norms of the males-only PGA circuit, Annika replied, "You've got to believe in yourself."

Self-expectations are such a powerful regulator of performance. You don't have to be a star athlete to know that how you think about yourself—your self-efficacy expectations—has everything to do with your ability to execute a course of action or attain a certain level of performance.

Your self-efficacy expectations are your perceptions of your ability to carry out your role. Research has consistently confirmed that the stronger people believe in their capabilities, the greater and more persistent they will be in their efforts and the longer they will persevere in the face of obstacles. Simply put, expectations regulate behavior. People tend to avoid tasks and situations that they believe exceed their capabilities and seek out activities they deem themselves capable of handling.

What are your self-expectations? What administrative tasks have you convinced yourself that you are great, okay, or lousy at? What myths do you perpetuate by telling others that you lack the talent or skill to achieve? Do you ever hear yourself saying things like "I'm no good at budgets" or "I'm no good at public speaking"? Negative expectations are a strong predictor of negative results. Researchers who study exceptional leaders find that regardless of the field or discipline, individuals who consistently achieve at high levels believe in themselves and set high expectations for themselves. Their most important characteristic, though, is that they concentrate on their strengths rather than focus on their limitations.

Your self-expectations are closely related to your overall attitude and how you handle adversity. Your attitude is your focus on life, the way you approach things mentally. If you view life's situations positively, you communicate to those around you that you welcome the challenges and responsibilities of leadership.

Positive attitude—that can-do spirit—is contagious and uplifting. Focusing on what's wrong in the world and the barriers and obstacles to progress can pull people down. In the face of genuine challenges, how you approach a situation can influence people's willingness to problem solve and be solution oriented. Leaders must be mindful of their thoughts and actions in the broader context of how they affect others, not just themselves.

P eople catch our attitudes just like they catch our colds.

*John Maxwell*

---

### Attitude

*We cannot choose how many years we will live, but we can*
*Choose how much life those years will have.*
*We cannot control the beauty of our face, but we can*
*Control the expression on it.*
*We cannot control life's difficult moments, but we can*
*Choose to make life less difficult.*
*We cannot control the negative atmosphere of the world,*
*But we can control the atmosphere of our minds.*
*Too often, we try to choose and control things we cannot.*
*Too seldom, we choose to control what we can ... our attitude.*

Anonymous.

## Do You Regularly Seek Feedback from Others?

Many of us have no idea how our actions are viewed or experienced by others. We may occasionally get unsolicited feedback about our behavior from our closest friends, family, or significant other, but we lack an understanding of how we come across to our colleagues in the work setting.

Asking for feedback and suggestions about how you can improve your performance can be scary. The process, however, is extraordinarily valuable in helping you become a stronger leader. Knowing how others perceive your actions helps you better understand the subtle but powerful ways you impact the quality of their work life. Knowing what they view as your strengths and your areas for improvement helps you become more responsive to their needs. And isn't that what leadership is all about?

> What a gift it is to see ourselves as others see us.
>
> *Robert Burns*

### Are You Ready?

To assess your readiness for engaging a multi-rater feedback process, ask yourself the following questions:

- Am I open to hearing how my actions affect others?

- Do I value input from those who work with me?

- Can I listen to feedback from others without getting defensive?

- Do I believe I could be a more effective manager?

- Do I agree not to retaliate for people telling me the truth as they see it?

- Am I willing to accept the perceptions that others have of my performance, even if I do not agree with them?

- Do I welcome honest and direct feedback?

- Do I understand that the intent behind my behavior may not be what others actually experience?

- Do I recognize that in order to improve my leadership, I must be willing to take action on feedback?

*Adapted from Jude-York, D., & Wise, S. (1997). Multipoint feedback: A 360° catalyst for change. Menlo Park, CA: Crisp.*

By collecting information from many people—your board, the center's owner, the executive director of your agency, your peers, the staff you supervise, and the parents of children in your program—you will benefit from multiple perspectives of how you act and are seen by others. Some refer to this approach as 360° feedback or multi-rater feedback. Whatever term you use, the more perspectives you solicit, the more complete the knowledge you will have about how others perceive your strengths and your areas for growth. This knowledge leads to insights about yourself that you may not have had.

Appendix B is a multi-rate leadership assessment you can use to elicit feedback from your colleagues. Feel free to adapt this instrument by adding additional questions that measure appropriate competencies, behaviors, or skills relating to your position or your organization. It is best to give the form only to individuals who have worked with you for a minimum of six months. Also, be sure to complete the assessment yourself. That way you can use the scores to compare your perceptions with the perceptions of your colleagues.

*LaToya is the owner and director of a small, for-profit child care center housed in a converted storefront in the business district of a low-income community. She supervises seven teachers and one office manager. LaToya attended a two-day leadership conference and was introduced to the concept of multi-rater evaluation. The workshop caused her to really reexamine her leadership assumptions, particularly with regard to the performance appraisal process.*

*LaToya had always viewed performance evaluation from a top-down perspective—that it was her job responsibility to evaluate others. It simply never occurred to her that performance feedback could be a two-way process. "To say I was nervous when I sent out a memo and survey to the staff inviting them to give some feedback on my leadership performance is an understatement," says LaToya. "I was absolutely terrified at the prospect that someone might be mean-spirited and say something nasty about me. How wrong I was. The process turned out to be the catalyst for an open discussion with staff members about how we all could support each other's professional growth."*

*LaToya was pleasantly surprised when she tabulated the survey results from the eight respondents and compared their average scores with that of her own assessment of her leadership abilities. Her staff identified most of the*

# Multi-Rater Summary Form

Name: LaToya B.

| Trait | Self Rating | Other Raters | | | | | | | | | | Average of other raters |
|---|---|---|---|---|---|---|---|---|---|---|---|---|
| | | A | B | C | D | E | F | G | H | | | |
| Accessible | 4 | 4 | 4 | 4 | 3 | 4 | 5 | 5 | 4 | | | 4.13 |
| Collaborative | 4 | 4 | 5 | 5 | 4 | 4 | 3 | 4 | 4 | | | 4.13 |
| Confident | 4 | 4 | 4 | 4 | 4 | 5 | 5 | 4 | 5 | | | 4.38 |
| Creative | 3 | 4 | 4 | 3 | 3 | 4 | 3 | 3 | 4 | | | 3.50 |
| Dependable | 4 | 4 | 4 | 4 | 4 | 5 | 5 | 4 | 5 | | | 4.38 |
| Direct | 3 | 3 | 3 | 4 | 3 | 4 | 4 | 3 | 4 | | | 3.50 |
| Empathetic | 5 | 5 | 5 | 5 | 4 | 5 | 5 | 5 | 5 | | | 4.88 |
| Enthusiastic | 4 | 4 | 5 | 5 | 4 | 4 | 3 | 4 | 4 | | | 4.13 |
| Ethical | 5 | 5 | 5 | 4 | 5 | 5 | 5 | 5 | 5 | | | 4.88 |
| Fair | 4 | 4 | 5 | 5 | 4 | 4 | 5 | 5 | 5 | | | 4.63 |
| Flexible | 4 | 5 | 5 | 5 | 5 | 4 | 5 | 5 | 5 | | | 4.88 |
| Friendly | 4 | 5 | 5 | 5 | 5 | 5 | 5 | 5 | 5 | | | 5.00 |
| A good listener | 5 | 5 | 5 | 5 | 5 | 4 | 5 | 5 | 5 | | | 4.88 |
| Inspiring | 4 | 4 | 5 | 5 | 4 | 4 | 3 | 4 | 4 | | | 4.13 |
| Knowledgeable | 5 | 5 | 5 | 5 | 5 | 5 | 5 | 5 | 5 | | | 5.00 |
| Objective | 4 | 4 | 5 | 5 | 4 | 4 | 3 | 5 | 4 | | | 4.25 |
| Open | 5 | 4 | 4 | 4 | 4 | 4 | 4 | 4 | 4 | | | 4.00 |
| Optimistic | 5 | 5 | 5 | 5 | 5 | 5 | 5 | 5 | 5 | | | 5.00 |
| Organized | 5 | 4 | 4 | 4 | 4 | 4 | 4 | 4 | 4 | | | 4.00 |
| Predictable | 4 | 5 | 5 | 5 | 4 | 5 | 4 | 5 | 5 | | | 4.75 |
| A problem solver | 4 | 4 | 5 | 5 | 4 | 4 | 5 | 5 | 4 | | | 4.50 |
| Resourceful | 5 | 4 | 4 | 3 | 4 | 4 | 4 | 4 | 5 | | | 4.00 |
| Respectful | 4 | 5 | 5 | 5 | 5 | 5 | 5 | 5 | 5 | | | 5.00 |
| Supportive | 4 | 4 | 5 | 5 | 4 | 4 | 3 | 4 | 4 | | | 4.13 |
| Visionary | 4 | 4 | 4 | 4 | 4 | 5 | 4 | 4 | 4 | | | 4.13 |
| **Total** | 106 | 108 | 115 | 113 | 104 | 110 | 107 | 111 | 113 | | | 110.19 |
| **Average rating** | 4.24 | 4.32 | 4.60 | 4.52 | 4.16 | 4.40 | 4.28 | 4.44 | 4.52 | | | 4.41 |

Agreed-upon strengths: empathetic, ethical, knowledgeable, good listener, optimistic

Unrealized strengths: flexible, friendly, predictable, respectful

Areas for growth: creative, direct

Blind spots: open, organized, resourceful

*same strengths that she saw in herself—that she was knowledgeable about the field, ethical in her conduct, optimistic in her outlook, empathetic in her approach with others, and a good listener. Her staff also agreed with her about two potential areas for growth—LaToya's need to become more direct in her oral and written communication ("not ramble so much" as one person noted in a marginal comment) and being open to more creative ways to solve problems. What really surprised LaToya, though, were the traits that staff rated her higher than she did herself (flexible, friendly, predictable, respectful). The knowledge that her staff viewed these traits as strengths really boosted her confidence.*

*There were three areas in which LaToya had rated herself higher than her staff rated her—being open in sharing important information about the center, knowing how to create organizational systems to ensure the smooth functioning of the center, and knowing how to tap community resources to get things done. While the discrepancy in scores was not large, the differences in perceptions helped LaToya realize that these were her blind spots. Looking at these traits through the eyes of her staff made her appreciate that their perception of what it meant to be open, organized, and resourceful differed somewhat from her perception.*

It is no surprise that people like to hear what is consistent with their own views and resist feedback that may be contrary to these views. By eliciting feedback from individuals who are your supervisors, by direct reports, and from clients you will get a more complete profile of how the people who interact with you in different capacities see you. Accept this input for what it is—their personal perceptions.

Your ability to handle less-than-flattering feedback is related to your level of self-confidence. If you are defensive in the face of criticism, then you should not initiate a 360° feedback process. But if you feel you can learn from others' perceptions and evaluations of your performance, you will benefit and grow from the experience. Search for the merit in others' opinions. Look for themes in what they share and be open to changing your style where appropriate.

# CHAPTER 4

# Becoming a Facilitative Leader

Facilitative leadership doesn't just happen. Directors who cultivate and sustain exemplary early care and education organizations do so by carefully tuning in to the needs of people, shaping individual and group expectations of what the center could be doing, and expanding perspectives so that all involved understand the complex nature of the collective work to be done. This chapter explores what it means to be a facilitative leader in early care and education. It gives you an opportunity to think about the ways you personally can create connections, shape expectations, and expand perspectives in your work setting.

## Creating Connections

An early childhood program is essentially an intricate network of social relationships. These relationships are the cement that holds a program together. When we think about relationships, three areas typically come to mind: child-child relationships, teacher-child relationships, and teacher-parent relationships. While positive peer relationships between children, solid and nurturing relationships between teachers and children, and close and caring connections between teachers and parents are essential in a quality child care program, they alone do not constitute a truly exemplary program.

Directors of exemplary programs have a broader view of relationships: they view them as the vehicle for establishing a sense of community—both inside and outside the center. This includes cultivating caring connections between teachers (teacher-teacher relationships), creating esprit de corps (staff-center relationships), and reaching out to the neighborhood and community (center-community relationships).

**Cultivating connections between teachers.** People who enter the field of early childhood are usually caring and compassionate. But the treadmill of activity that consumes their time and energy on the job may keep them from establishing close relationships with one another. The physical layout of space, time pressures, and conflicting schedules are just some of the obstacles that prevent staff from exchanging information, sharing ideas, and lending and receiving support.

The teacher-teacher relationships in many child care centers mirror what we see in children's parallel play—although they are in close proximity, they go about their daily routine of activities pretty much in isolation. Organizational theorists describe this phenomenon as a *loosely coupled organizational structure*. In loosely coupled centers teachers work independently, carrying out their respective jobs. Classroom activities and interactions with the children are central to their focus and job satisfaction. Interpersonal relationships with other staff are marginal.

Loosely coupled organizational structures are good in that they tend to meet teacher needs for independence and autonomy in decision making. But they can also cause feelings of isolation, an air of competition, and a lack of opportunities for collaboration and learning from others.

We often forget that what most people want more than anything is the chance to belong and make a difference in something they value. Belonging is more than just being involved; it is feeling valued. There is an old saying: "A little kindness from person to person is better than a vast love for all of humankind." Translated into child care terms, it means that teachers must first feel connected to one another before they can feel a sense of connection to the center.

Your role as leader is to consciously looks for ways to cultivate closeness in the work environment. A sense of community on the job not only provides the social support that nourishes the spirit, it also provides the impetus that makes individuals strive for optimal performance. People engaged in supportive relationships cope better with stress in their professional and personal lives. Teachers who have good relationships with each other model this behavior to children. The following are a few ways directors can promote greater collegiality in their centers.

- Arrange work schedules to facilitate collaboration between teachers for planning projects, team teaching, visiting other centers, and attending conferences together.
- Encourage joint field trips, sharing of curriculum materials among classrooms, and carpooling among staff.
- Ensure that the performance appraisal system of the center values how well individuals support one another as a measure of their performance.
- Encourage and support mentoring relationships with time, resources, and schedules.
- Make sure a teachers' lounge is available where teachers can meet, talk, laugh, commiserate, eat, and work together.
- Set up a staff bulletin board where teachers can exchange teaching tips and information.
- Highlight staff accomplishments in your center's newsletter.

- Keep the staff roster up-to-date and distribute or post a birthday list.
- Schedule periodic social events to which staff can bring their families and socialize on a more relaxed basis.

**We're in this together—Nurturing that esprit de corps.** Satisfying and fulfilling co-worker relationships are a prerequisite for achieving a group identity—that esprit de corps that is the hallmark of a high-functioning team. Looking at connections from this perspective means you need to consciously think about the center culture and how to strengthen your staff's connection to the broader mission of the center.

The culture of exemplary child care programs is characterized by a climate of trust and openness and a shared belief that achieving group goals transcends individual wishes. So how do you go about creating a strong center culture that promotes quality practices and synergy in working relationships? Here are a few suggestions:

- Encourage open communication and the expression of diverse points of view. Walter Lipmann once said, "When everyone thinks alike, no one thinks very much." In your leadership role, you can model behavior that is accepting of differing points of view.
- Structure numerous opportunities for teachers to talk about the deeper philosophical issues relating to early care and education. The activities described in Chapter 2 relating to personal and collective values is a good place to start.
- Use the terms *we* and *our* in your everyday language to communicate a sense of connection. These are words of inclusion, cooperation, and alliance—the essence of community.
- Seize every opportunity to tie individual success to group success, emphasizing not only individual accomplishments, but also how those accomplishments advance the goals of the center.
- Communicate information broadly to ensure that people are kept well informed. Err on the side of information overload.
- Regularly solicit feedback on teachers' perceptions about how well the program functions. You can construct your own informal assessment to do this or if you want to ensure anonymity and promote more candid feedback, you can use the *Early Childhood Work Environment Survey* available from the Center for Early Childhood Leadership (www.nl.edu/cecl).
- Schedule time at staff meetings to do team-building activities. Include opportunities for staff to expand their understanding of different learning styles and how to communicate and collaborate based on these styles.

- Delegate some of your administrative tasks. Seasoned teachers can serve as hosts for prospective parents visiting the program or be on hand to monitor the facility when outside groups rent space. They can also represent the center at public hearings or community meetings relating to child care issues.

- Invite teachers to your board meetings. Likewise, encourage (even require) that board members periodically spend time at the center to get to know the staff.

- Celebrate who you are as a center. If a teacher has a special talent for scrapbooking, provide some release time and the materials to create a pictorial history of your center, highlighting special events, traditions, and celebrations in the center's history. Keep this scrapbook on display in your reception area.

**Reaching out—Connecting with the community.** If you want to build a strong culture and a sense of community, your relationships within the center constitute only part of the equation. You also need to consider how your center connects with the immediate neighborhood and the local community of which it is a part.

External relationships are the easiest to neglect. With the frenetic pace of everyday life, directors often lament that they just don't have time to make the community linkages they should. But the payoff is worthwhile. Directors who broaden their circle of relationships to build strong community connections report a lower incidence of vandalism at their centers, fewer problems in recruiting volunteers and prospective staff, and longer wait lists.

No doubt you and your teachers are already making important contacts in the community—arranging class field trips to a local business, soliciting in-kind donations from neighborhood merchants, making referrals for children at community mental health and social service agencies, lobbying for local ordinances that affect children and families, and contacting your local resource and referral agency to update program information.

The important point is not how often contacts are made, but how impressions about the program are shaped by those contacts. In other words, do those contacts promote a positive image of the center and help build a sound reputation for the program? Talk with your staff about the importance of every community contact they make; encourage them to think of themselves as ambassadors representing the center. Here are some strategies for ensuring positive community relations:

- Remind staff regularly about first impressions. Because first impressions are powerful in shaping people's opinions about the program, it is important that every visitor and telephone contact be treated with respect. Think of the multiplying effect if each person speaks positively about your program to a dozen or so other people.

- Keep your immediate neighbors happy. The appearance of the facility, noise level, and traffic patterns are particularly important issues for neighbors. Keep them informed when you plan to sponsor a special event at the center. Invite them to volunteer and put them on your newsletter mailing list.

- Be active in community organizations and participate on community boards (e.g., Rotary, Chamber of Commerce). Put together a five- to ten-minute PowerPoint presentation or slide show about the center to present at community functions. Always take along brochures and business cards.

- Whenever public officials in the community take action in support of children and families, use the center's stationery to commend them. In the months preceding a local election, host a forum at the center for parents to meet the candidates and hear how they stand on issues relating to children and families.

- Provide workshops and lectures for parents in the community. If you do not have the staff or expertise to do this, then allow your center to be used by other groups hosting such events.

- Make connections with the early childhood instructors at the local community college. These contacts can pay off in rich dividends. Offer the center as a site for students doing field observations.

## Shaping Expectations

While we may be in the people business, we are also in the knowledge business. And that means connecting people with information about best practices and promoting an understanding that the exchange of ideas and resources is a core characteristic of the center. Staff expectations regarding this knowledge enterprise will influence the program's social atmosphere and staff members' impact on children and families. Shaping expectations begins with shifting the focus from teaching to learning at all levels of the organization, consciously structuring language expectations, and building a program based on exploiting people's strengths rather than accommodating their weaknesses.

**Shifting the focus from teaching to learning.** The best early childhood programs are learning communities not just for children but also for adults—a place where people come together with a shared purpose of constructing new understandings together. A learning community is a place where collective aspirations are set free, new patterns of thinking are nurtured, and the organization expands its capacity for constructive and innovative problem solving.

H igh expectations don't get communicated by wishful thinking.

*Barry Posner*

A learning community is not just a place; it is also a state of mind. It is a philosophy of teamwork that embraces the notion that multiple points of view on any topic are important and that the synergistic effect of exploring new ideas together yields greater dividends than sharing concrete facts or information.

The early childhood programs of Reggio Emilia, Italy provide a wonderful case study of learning communities in action—where children, teachers, and parents are involved in sharing ideas, engaging in active dialogue, and constructing new meanings. Reggio programs recognize that everyone is an active participant in the educational enterprise, with each person contributing complementary and necessary knowledge.

You don't need to go to Italy to create this kind of active learning community. You can shape individual and collective expectations for engaged learning and continuous improvement right in your own program if you make a conscious effort. Here are some suggestions to get you started:

- Help people define what *best practice* means in the context of your program.
- Facilitate the flow of information throughout the center.
- Encourage the admission of ignorance and help seeking.
- Cultivate norms of respectful listening.
- Structure opportunities for collaborative planning.
- Support mentoring relationships at all levels of the organization.
- Focus meetings around the exchange of ideas and sharing of new instructional strategies.
- Encourage "What if ..." questions.
- When things don't go as planned, ask, "What can we learn from this situation?"
- Help teachers master the art of reflective practice.

In her research, Sara Lawrence Lightfoot has found that the key factor distinguishing good schools from truly exemplary schools is staffs' willingness to look at their imperfections and create a climate of continual improvement. What she describes in these exemplary educational settings is a learning community—a place where teachers and administrative staff engage in frequent, continuous, and precise talk about programmatic issues. They plan, design, prepare, research, and evaluate together. But most important, these programs have built-in mechanisms that allow staff to regularly reflect on their performance, evaluate feedback, and examine new and alternative practices.

The best time and place to nurture the norms of a learning community are in your regularly scheduled staff meetings. Take advantage of these opportunities together to extend people's understanding of new research in child development and innovative teaching practices, and to share feedback about different instructional strategies. The book *Making the Most of Meetings* has many ideas on how to plan and facilitate meetings that promote this kind of meaningful professional development.

**Norms of communication—What we say and how we say it.** Shaping expectations also means shaping how people communicate with one another at work—norms of communication. As director, you more than anyone else can influence these norms.

If you have never thought of yourself as a language leader, do this simple exercise. For one whole day take note of the conversations that go on at your center. Pay close attention to the types of conversations people have—the topics they discuss and the tone or emotional context of their exchanges. Linguist Deborah Tannen is fond of saying that each person's life is lived in a series of conversations. Our words are important because they create our consciousness—the things we pay attention to. What do staff conversations tell you about the culture of your center?

The language of complaint permeates many (perhaps even most) work environments. In fact, complaining is often the common bond that connects employees who share a sense of disappointment, unhappiness, and even resentment about their jobs. They may complain how their work is structured, how their co-workers annoy them, or how their supervisors are neglectful of their basic needs. Regardless of the cause, complaining saps people's vitality and potential and keeps them locked in a culture of dissatisfaction.

Think about the norms of communication at your center—the content and tone of people's conversations. How much complaining goes on? Is your staff lounge a major groan zone for airing frustrations?

As director you have a range of possible responses when people come to you with complaints. You can listen and empathize, letting them know that you understand and will try to accommodate their concerns by changing this or that. Or you can try to help them see the big picture, altering their view of the situation with additional information so that the reasons for their complaints disappear.

While these are both time-honored strategies, they usually fall short of changing the individual or the situation that precipitated the complaint. We may be disappointed to find that people continue to complain about the same issues or even more annoyed when they come up with a litany of new gripes and concerns.

The problem with the language of complaint is that it only tells us what people don't like, what they can't stand. It doesn't reveal what they are committed to, the values and deeply held convictions that cause them to feel frustrated when things don't go their way.

A more powerful strategy is helping people reshape their expectations of themselves, moving them from a mind-set of blame to a mind-set of personal responsibility. The goal is helping individuals understand those things they are committed to—what they stand for. It means helping people shift from being a victim and feeling disappointed, complaining, critical and wishing life were better, to being proactive and empowered to articulate what is important to them and then working to create a work environment that embodies those values. Here are some things you can do to shape language expectations:

- Be authentic in your conversations. The best leaders talk with people, not at them.

- Help staff understand that the way they talk to one another is as important as what they talk about. Courtesy and respect are the hallmarks of a caring collegial environment.

- Model positive intentionality by always presuming that others' motives and intentions are honorable.

- Recognize the power of every conversation you have. Your level of optimism or defeatism creates expectations for your staff. If you aren't positive and hopeful, why should they be?

- Realize it is not your job to make everyone happy. When a complaint is lodged or a concern presented, respond by saying "How can I help you solve this issue?" not "How can I solve this issue for you?"

- Help people understand they are the architects of their own realities. Sometimes this means coming to terms with the realization that the program may not be the right fit for them.

- Share with your staff responsibility for budget-driven tough decisions. Help them understand that the nature of child care is such that there will *never* be enough staff, enough time, enough materials, or enough space. Share information and make them partners in issues relating to resource allocation.

**Building a strengths-based organization.** Many directors treat staff like a broken kitchen appliance—find out what's wrong with the dang thing and fix it. They spend precious professional development dollars identifying their staff's weaknesses and trying to fix them. Focusing on deficits is not unique to early childhood organizations. In workplaces around the world, people are encouraged to identify, analyze, and correct their weaknesses in order to become better.

Treat people as if they were what they ought to be and you help them to become what they are capable of being.

*Goethe*

Most organizations take their employees' strengths for granted and focus supervisory and professional development resources on minimizing weaknesses, those areas where people need to become proficient.

The Gallup Organization considers this management approach to be based on two flawed assumptions: that every person can become competent in almost anything and that each person's greatest potential for growth lies in his or her identified areas of weakness. In its Strengthsfinder project, Gallup proposes that a strengths-based organization is built on two positive assumptions: that each person's strengths are enduring and that each person's greatest potential for growth is in the areas of his or her identified strengths.

A strengths-based organization is built on the premise that individuals will excel by cultivating and maximizing their strengths rather than fixing their weaknesses. This makes good sense, considering what we know from adult learning theory and motivation theory. To build an exemplary child care program, directors create opportunities for teachers to identify their passions and then allow them the space and resources to pursue them.

A strength is an area of performance in which an individual excels and does so consistently. It is also an area in which a person experiences intrinsic satisfaction. Gallup defines a strength as a combination of talents (those naturally recurring patterns of thought, feelings, or behaviors), knowledge (facts and lessons learned), and skills (the how to or steps of an activity).

So how can you shape expectations by building a strengths-based early care and education program? Here are a few suggestions to get you started:

- Introduce the concept of strengths at the first job interview you have with a prospective employee. Ask, "What talents, skills, special competencies, and unique contributions would you bring to this center?"

- Provide opportunities for staff to talk about and celebrate their strengths. Help them become aware of one another's unique strengths.

- At least once a year, ask your staff these questions:
  "Do you have the opportunity every day to do what you do best?"
  "What resources do you need to excel in your job?"
  "What part of your job do you enjoy most and want to do more of?"
  "What task would you rather do more than any other?"

- Encourage staff to think about how their job descriptions and role expectations could be expanded or redefined to maximize their strengths.

- Develop a strengths profile of your entire center. Share this profile with your staff, and ask them to think about how the information could be used in hiring new staff who would add to and complement those already on board.

> The best advice is not to focus on your strengths and ignore your weaknesses, but rather, to focus on your strengths and find ways to manage your weaknesses.
>
> *Marcus Buckingham*

## Expanding Perspectives

You've probably heard the tale of the six blind men standing around an elephant, each feeling a different part of the animal. One touched the trunk and announced that an elephant was like a snake. Another took hold of the tusk and compared an elephant to a spear. Another felt the leg, declaring that an elephant was like a tree trunk. Still another placed his hands on the side of the elephant and exclaimed that the beast was like a wall. The fifth, holding the elephant's ear, compared the animal to a large fan. The last blind man took hold of the tail and announced that an elephant was like a rope. John Saxe's poem concludes:

> And so these men of Indostan
> Disputed loud and long,
> Each in his own opinion,
> Exceeding stiff and strong.
> Though each was partly in the right,
> And all were in the wrong.

It is such a simple notion that we all perceive the world differently; yet we often act like the blind men of Indostan, firmly convinced that our view of the world is the one and only truth. How blind we are in recognizing the validity and value of different perspectives and points of view. Our perceptions become our reality—the only reality.

**Different realities.** The process of perceiving the world and making sense of it is highly personal. Each of us observes different things and focuses our attention on different aspects of what we see. In the world of perception, the same thing can mean something entirely different to different people. Our deeply held values and past experiences strongly impact what we focus on, how we make sense of what we experience, and the meaning we attach to different events.

We each have separate realities about the world because we each take in different information and then interpret the information in our unique way. The irony is that once we have formed an initial impression about a situation, a person, or an event, we tend to look for evidence to support our view, and end up filtering out information that might contradict it.

Think about of the magazines and journals you subscribe to, the lectures you attend, or the radio talk shows you listen to. My guess is they all fit a pattern reinforcing your beliefs and point of view about the world. Seldom do we take time to read articles, attend lectures, or listen to broadcasters who would challenge us to think about the world in different ways. Seldom do we get out of our comfort zone to look at the world through different eyes.

Our perceptions shape our paradigms about the world. A paradigm is the lens we use to filter new information and the data we take in. It is a model or scheme that helps us organize and understand something better. People experience a paradigm shift when they get married, become parents, or learn they have a serious illness. Think about your promotion from teacher to director. No doubt you experienced a paradigm shift in the way you viewed your role, the scope of your responsibility, and the nature of your co-worker relationships. Paradigm shifts cause us to view the same world in a dramatically different way.

**Three perspectives.** When we talk about point of view, it is helpful to think of three different types of perspectives: egocentric, allocentric, and macrocentric. An *egocentric perspective* is our own unique point of view, shaped by our past experiences, cognitive capacity, deeply held values, and formal education.

As early childhood educators we are familiar with the term egocentrism as an important developmental stage of early childhood. Children in the preoperational stage of cognitive development believe that everyone thinks as they think and acts as they act for the same reasons. But egocentrism doesn't disappear as children move into the concrete operations stage of cognitive development. It is part of our cognitive process across the life span.

Adults are often guilty of narrow, egocentric thinking. We have difficulty seeing clearly someone else's point of view and perceive our perspective to be the only valid one. If you've traveled to England, did you ever say, "Why do these people have to drive on the *wrong* side of the road?" If you've traveled to France, did you ever think, "Everyone here speaks a *foreign* language."

W e all live under the same sky, but we don't all have the same horizon.

*Konrad Adenauer*

"I've been talking too much. Your turn. Tell me what you think about what I said..."

An *allocentric perspective* is being able to see another person's point of view. The root *allo* means *other*. An allocentric perspective allows us to experience empathy for others; to be able to "get inside their skin" and feel what they feel. Developing an allocentric perspective takes skill and patience. It involves deep listening—really trying to see the world through a different lens. As a director, you can help expand your staff's allocentric capacities by asking them questions that move them out of their narrow perceptual frames.

*Isabelle is the director of a small center that offers full-day care for 35 children. She has a staff of four teachers, all of whom are young and unmarried. Four days before Christmas, one of Isabelle's teachers, Maria, gives a cool, detached greeting to Nathan's mother when she drops him off in the morning. Isabelle thinks this is uncharacteristic of Maria, so she asks her if she had a run-in with Nathan's mom.*

*"No," replies Maria. "I just think Nathan's mom is neglectful. She leaves him here every day for 10 hours and on these two days that she has off from work, I think she should keep Nathan home with her. I just know she dumped him here so she could go Christmas shopping today."*

*Isabelle understands that the anger behind Maria's judgment of Nathan's mom is probably due to feelings of resentment because her own mother left her with babysitters more often than she liked. Isabelle seizes the moment to help expand Maria's egocentric perspective of the situation: "It sounds like you have some strong feelings that working mothers should not leave their children with us when they have the day off. In your mind, what would be some legitimate reasons why Nathan's mom might want him here today, despite the fact that she has the day off from work?"*

*This open-ended, nonthreatening question helps Maria think of some alternative reasons that working mothers might need child care even on their day off. "Maybe she feels that Nathan would be more entertained here than being dragged around a mall for eight hours," Maria says. She adds, "It's also possible that she has been working so hard that she might just need a day to herself to sleep and rest." After a thoughtful pause, Maria concludes, "I guess it's not right for me to judge her reasons, whatever they are. My job is to support her and provide a safe and good environment for Nathan while he is here."*

Finally, a *macrocentric perspective* is being able to see the big picture—how one's actions intersect with those of others. It is like viewing the landscape from above, a bird's-eye view. Have you ever driven in the fast lane of an expressway behind a driver going only 40 miles per hour who is oblivious to the fact that other motorists are flashing their lights and passing on the right? The motorist lacks a macrocentric perspective, the ability to see how his actions impact those around him.

A macrocentric perspective is not easily achieved. It requires having the capacity to be part of the picture while simultaneously being able to step outside of it and see all the connecting elements. Consider, for example, the teacher who asks you for a raise, "a measly 25 cents an hour more." From the teacher's perspective, that quarter seems like a reasonable request. From your perspective, however, it is clear the teacher has a limited understanding of the big picture. A small raise of 25 cents per hour for one person can have big ramifications regarding compensation equity for other staff and maintaining the center's delicate balance between revenue and expenses.

**Closing the gap.** At work and at home, most interpersonal problems exist because one person's reality isn't another person's reality. Disagreements that escalate into all-out conflict seldom have to do with facts; they almost always have to do with differences in perception about the meaning and importance of different events. The changing landscape of ethnically, linguistically, and culturally diverse populations served by early childhood programs only adds to the potential for misunderstanding.

What this means is that leaders of early care and education programs must have the ability and skill to help people understand and appreciate the value of different perspectives. Here are a few things you can do:

- Help teachers suspend judgment on what they observe. When most of us observe children or adults in different situations, our tendency is to evaluate the observed behavior by the "goodness" of what we see. In other words, is the behavior consistent with our way of doing things? Instead, encourage staff to ask, "How can I account for what I am observing?" Why is this person doing or saying what he or she is doing or saying?

> Each of us tends to see things in ways that take our own interests disproportionately into account.
>
> *Roger Fisher*

- Model tolerance. To be tolerant, one must embrace the notion that different points of view are not only important, they are essential in growing, thriving organizations. Tolerance goes hand in hand with flexibility—a willingness to consider that there is often more than one solution to a problem.

- Engage in learning conversations. A learning conversation begins with the premise that we each have something to gain from hearing the other's opinions on an issue. "Share with me your feelings about this issue" or "Help me understand your perspective regarding this situation" are good ways to launch a learning conversation.

- Help staff disentangle *intent* from *impact*. We have all made the mistake of assuming that we understand someone else's intentions. Not surprisingly, we are often wrong in the assumptions we make. We infer intentions from the impact that an action or behavior has had on us. And frequently we assume the worst. Intentions are invisible. It is only through a learning conversation that we can really understand someone's intent.

- Encourage staff to read books and articles with different points of view from their own. For a lively staff meeting, engage in role-play activities in which staff defend positions contrary to their own beliefs and point of view.

- Embrace diversity as an organizational goal. Working with colleagues who have different backgrounds, family traditions, and experiences broadens people's frames of reference and exposes them to new ways of thinking. If you recruit and hire as diverse a staff as possible with respect to gender, ethnic, linguistic, and cultural differences, you increase the group's potential for personal insight and growth.

- Help staff see that most innovative ideas come from borrowing, adding, or combining old ones. Being open to modifying one's way of looking at the world offers possibilities for new and better ways of doing things.

## My Commitment to Action

Take a moment now to complete Exercise 7 and reflect on ways that you can build your capacity as a facilitative leader by making connections, shaping expectations, and expanding perspectives.

N othing is more dangerous than an idea when it is the only one you have

*E. Chartier*

## Creating Connections

- Things I can do to foster connections between teachers:

  _____

- Things I can do to nurture an esprit de corps and greater connection to the center:

  _____

- Things I can do to strengthen connections between the center and the community:

  _____

## Shaping Expectations

- Things I can do to shift the focus from teaching to learning:

  _____

- Things I can do to foster positive norms of communication:

  _____

- Things I can do to build a strengths-based organization:

  _____

## Expanding Perspectives

- Things I can do to help staff understand the concept of different realities:

  _____

- Things I can do to promote allocentric and macrocentric perspective taking:

  _____

- Things I can do to help close the gap when differing perspectives exist:

  _____

# CHAPTER 5

# Bumper Stickers to Live By

You've probably had the experience of humming down the interstate looking at the scenery and not thinking about anything in particular, when out of the corner of your eye you spot a bumper sticker that catches your attention. Sometimes it's a phrase that captures a profound philosophical truth. Other times it's a humorous play on words that sends you into hoots of laughter. Still other times it's a political slogan for a beloved or belittled candidate. People use bumpers stickers to proclaim, pronounce, profess, and protest.

In this chapter we'll summarize the lessons of effective leadership in ten easy-to-remember bumper stickers. Some are well-known expressions—pithy truisms that capture the wisdom of good leaders. Others are corny phrases designed to make you think about your job in new and different ways. In either case, these bumper stickers are designed to capture the deeper significance of what it means to be a leader in the context of your early childhood work setting.

## "Quality Is a Moving Target"

For centuries parents and caregivers routinely put babies on their tummies to sleep. For decades preschool included peanut butter as a lunchtime staple. Today both these practices are considered inappropriate and potentially harmful to young children in group care. No doubt you can think of a dozen other examples where what you once thought was right was turned upside down.

If you are a seasoned director, you have experienced firsthand how advances in the fields of neuroscience, law, psychology, medicine, economics, nutrition, and education have greatly impacted your understanding of what constitutes best practice in early care and education. Issues like what to feed children; how to ensure their safety; how to organize learning environments that promote optimal cognitive, social, and emotional growth; and how to best serve children with disabilities or cultural and linguistic differences are regularly reexamined in light of new findings from research and practice.

Quality is not a static concept. Some things we used to feel certain about, we now discard as antiquated, inappropriate, or even harmful. So what's a director to do? How do you go about setting goals and standards for best practice at your program knowing that tomorrow they may be obsolete?

The answer comes from the concept of positive uncertainty, a term coined by psychologist H. B. Gelatt. *Positive uncertainty* is an approach to decision making about the future when you don't know what it will be. It involves combining a traditional, linear, rational approach to decision making with a creative, nonlinear, and intuitive approach in order to evaluate new knowledge and ideas in light of your own social and cultural experience. It means feeling comfortable knowing that what is important and right to do at any one time, as you understand it, may change.

Positive uncertainty is premised on the belief that change is a vital and necessary ingredient in the administration of early childhood programs. The challenge for you as director is how to encourage norms of continuous improvement so that change can be incorporated into the life of your program without causing chaos. This is especially difficult for novice directors who desperately want things to be predictable, stable, and calm. Becoming a master director in large part rests on your ability to have one foot firmly grounded in the present while the other is poised to step into the future. Here are a few things you can do to instill norms of continuous improvement in your program:

- Keep your antennae up. Stay current with new developments in the field.

- Don't embrace every innovation that comes down the pike. Evaluate new ideas critically in light of research, the social and cultural context of your program, and your core values.

- Regularly ask staff, "Is there another way we might do this?" "How can we improve what we are doing?"

- Encourage staff to keep current about research on different issues. Designate different teachers as "resident experts" on various topics.

- Engage in brainstorming activities where wacky and wild suggestions are welcomed.

- Show your staff you are open to modifying your beliefs: "I used to think that ..., now I believe that ..."

- Spend time talking about the behaviors and practices classified in different quality levels of early childhood programming—*substandard, good enough,* and *exemplary*. What does child care look, sound, and feel like at each of these levels of quality?

## "Different Strokes for Different Folks "

The cornerstone of our work in early childhood education rests on the notion that all children are different. They come to us with unique developmental patterns, experiences, abilities, and backgrounds. In our work with adults, however, we sometimes lose sight of the importance of this same principle. The teachers and support staff who work in our early childhood programs also have different abilities, needs, values, and expectations. The unique set of factors that contributes to one teacher's job satisfaction will be quite different from those of another teacher working in the same center.

In child care centers across America we see cookie-cutter approaches to supervision and staff development—a one-size-fits-all mentality. It is no surprise that the turnover rate for teaching and support staff in early childhood programs is so high. If you couple the poor wages staff receive with the lack of individualized models of supervision and staff development, it is little wonder that teachers quit their jobs at such high rates. Some move to other centers in the hope of finding a more fulfilling fit. Most, however, leave the field disillusioned. Many who stay say they are just putting in time, going through the motions and getting through the day—no zest, no commitment, no personal satisfaction.

Effective directors live by the platinum rule—treat people the way they wish to be treated. In other words, they find out what things people value, and they structure work around those motivations. They understand that the job doesn't make the person; the person makes the job. They don't try to mold a person to a job description, but rather they build on a person's strengths and interests to craft a job description that reflects the uniqueness of that person.

Take a moment now to complete Exercise 8 on page 70. This exercise gives you an opportunity to think about the job factors that contribute to your own job satisfaction—those things that motivate you the most—and then to think about the job factors that are important in motivating the teachers on your staff.

Reflect on the insights you gleaned from completing this exercise. Some directors find that it is difficult to complete the section on their teachers; that they simply do not know what job factors are key motivators for their staff. Other directors realize that the teachers they have the easiest time working with are those whose motivators are most similar to their own. Surprise, surprise!

Uncovering the job factors that motivate your staff is the first step in structuring work conditions that are both satisfying and fulfilling to them. The next step is working one-on-one with them to personalize the information ("What does creativity mean to you?" How can we make sure opportunities for creativity are

All good leaders of people know what makes each person on their team "tick" as well as what gets them "ticked off."

*Michael Brandwein*

There is nothing so unequal as the equal treatment of unequals.
*Ken Blanchard*

69

embedded in your job?"). A leader knows that embracing the philosophy of *different strokes for different folks* is a win/win proposition. If you can satisfy people's needs to be creative (to achieve, to fulfill their potential, to master new skills), you and your center reap the benefits.

Different people value different aspects of their work. Below is a list of some of the ways jobs can be rewarding. Put a check (✓) next to the three job factors that motivate you the most. Then in the columns under the heading *Teacher*, put the initials of five of your teachers. Complete the exercise with each of them in mind. What job factors are most important in motivating each of them?

| Motivates me | Job Factor | Teacher | | | | |
|---|---|---|---|---|---|---|
| | | | | | | |
| | **Colleagues**—working with people you like | | | | | |
| | **Altruism**—helping others | | | | | |
| | **Achievement**—that feeling of accomplishment from doing a job well | | | | | |
| | **Pay**—earning a good living to buy the things you need | | | | | |
| | **Intellectual stimulation**—learning new things | | | | | |
| | **Variety**—the opportunity to do different kinds of things | | | | | |
| | **Challenge**—the opportunity to master new skills | | | | | |
| | **Security**—the assurance that your position is secure | | | | | |
| | **Creativity**—developing new ideas, creating new things | | | | | |
| | **Autonomy**—being independent in making decisions | | | | | |
| | **Recognition**—respect and acknowledgement from others | | | | | |
| | **Environment**—pleasant surroundings in which to work | | | | | |
| | **Leadership**—the opportunity to guide and influence the work of others | | | | | |
| | **Promotion**—opportunity for advancement | | | | | |
| | **Other:** | | | | | |

Leaders do not create motivation out of thin air. They unlock or channel existing motives.

*John Gardner*

*From Bloom, P. J., Sheerer, M., & Britz, J. (1991).* Blueprint for action: Achieving center-based change through staff development *(p. 238). Lake Forest, IL: New Horizons. Reprinted with permission.*

## "Don't Get Stuck in the Muck"

Directors who pursue center accreditation are often frustrated by how long it takes. They enter the self-study process with the notion that achieving accreditation is a linear step-by-step sequence. Do *a, b, c,* and *d* and *voila!* you're ready to submit your materials and host a validation visit. How surprised they are to find that each step in the self-study process surfaces new tasks to be done—program practices that need to be corrected, handbooks that need to be updated, policies and procedures that need to be reviewed. The goal of achieving accreditation then becomes overwhelming. Their initial enthusiasm for the task quickly evaporates and their box of self-study materials ends up in the supply closet behind the paint and construction paper. They are stuck in the muck.

Sound familiar? Every director gets stuck in the muck occasionally. The accreditation self-study process is but one example. Just too much to do and too little time to do it. For some directors these occasions represent a temporary setback, a chance to reconnoiter and make a new game plan. For others, however, a paralysis of the spirit seems to set in and good intentions are never realized. Teachers in these programs complain that issues don't seem to get resolved and the same topics are discussed over and over at staff meetings.

One of the defining characteristics of effective leaders is their ability to maintain a forward momentum in their organizations. They have created a climate of expectations, a task orientation, and specific strategies to manage people's time so that momentum is maintained in achieving both short- and long-term goals. If maintaining momentum is an issue for you, here are some things to consider:

**Let go of your need for perfection.** Many people have a compelling desire to do a job perfectly or not at all. But striving for perfection is not the same as striving for excellence. Perfectionism comes from setting unrealistically high standards. Sounds noble, but instead of motivating us, it tends to paralyze us. It takes courage to be less than perfect. If we are going to avoid getting stuck in the muck, we must tackle head on our devotion to over-organization, over-cleanliness, and over-conscientiousness. We must expose them for what they are—roadblocks to performance. Strive instead for functional efficiency and accept that you do not have to be a model of perfection to do a job you can take pride in.

**Avoid one-right-answer thinking.** Another reason directors get stuck in the muck is they assume there is one *best* answer or one *right* way to solve a problem. This kind of thinking can lead to a paralysis of analysis where you spend unnecessary time looking for more data or confirming evidence for the best solution. The fact is that for most of the organizational issues confronting early care and education programs, there are multiple right answers—multiple right ways to state policies, implement procedures, and evaluate progress. One-right-answer thinking stifles creativity and tends to immobilize.

**Divide and conquer.** It is often the enormity of a task that fuels procrastination and the feeling of being stuck. We tell ourselves, "I'll wait until I get a block of uninterrupted time to tackle this one" or "I haven't got all the materials I need." Accomplished project managers know that the only way to not feel overwhelmed by major projects is to break them down into manageable small tasks and then create a time line and system of accountability to ensure that each step is completed.

The big jobs in child care administration—accreditation self-study, writing a parent handbook, designing an orientation process, planning a fundraiser, developing a marketing plan—all lend themselves to this divide-and-conquer approach. When directors deliberately plan a strategy of small wins, they are usually far more successful in maintaining morale and momentum, both necessary elements in completing big jobs. Take a look at the book *Making the Most of Meetings* for some examples of forms and project planning strategies that will help you divide and conquer your big jobs.

**Don't try to achieve agreement on every issue.** Consensus is a powerful decision-making tool in program administration, but some directors confuse consensus with unanimity. They believe everyone must agree wholeheartedly with a decision before plans can move ahead. As a result, nothing happens.

While you will want to strive for unanimous support for your center improvement initiatives, most likely you will have to settle for something less—acceptance. Consensus means that all points of view have been heard and that everyone in the group accepts the decision. It also means that there will probably be a full range of opinions about any issue from unbridled enthusiasm to passive acceptance, and that is okay. If you are going to be known as an action-oriented leader, one who is able to maintain a positive momentum for your program improvement efforts, then you need to be comfortable with the knowledge that not everyone will be as gung ho as you are about different issues.

## "Simplicity Is Power"

Simplicity is the art of doing less of what doesn't matter and focusing more on what does matter. Effective directors strive for substance over bureaucracy. They keep memos short, policies crisp, words to a minimum. They go for the essence. They are constantly looking for ways to streamline their programs without compromising quality.

I have been told that the employee handbook for Nordstrom, a specialty store with a reputation for extraordinary customer service, consists of a small card that reads: "Our number one goal is to provide outstanding customer service.

*The most efficient and effective route to bold change is the participation of everyone, everyday in incremental change.*

*Tom Peters*

Set both your personal and professional goals high. We have great confidence in your ability to achieve them.  Rule #1: Use your good judgment in all situations." Nordstrom has mastered the concept of keeping it simple.

One of the hopes for the computer age was that small businesses would be able to become paperless work environments.  That has been hardly the case.  Most directors report that despite computerizing many of their office tasks and functions, they are dealing with more paper than ever before.

Take time to do a paper inventory of your office operations.  Ameritech did this a few years ago.  They created a financial reporting team made up of controllers and accountants.  The team roamed around, asking, "Do you really need those financial reports?"  They found that one employee spent five days each month preparing a 25-page report that no one read.  When it had completed it's in-house inventory, the team had eliminated six million pages of reports.

If you are serious about embracing the wisdom of the bumper sticker "Simplicity Is Power," here are a few things you can do:

- Meet with your office staff to think of ways you can reduce the amount of paper generated and routed to others.
- Ask your team, "What things are we doing today that if we were not already doing them, we would not start doing?"
- Create standard templates for forms, memos, newsletters, and minutes, and keep paper communications lean to reduce the amount of mental clutter people have to wade through to get to the essence of your message.
- Cut red tape for your teachers.  Eliminate the obstacles to their success.  This may mean reducing the number of signatures needed for small purchases or the number of copies needed for filing standard reports.
- Don't allow things to accumulate that no longer have a real function.  This means being selective about using your storage space.

## "Keep That Duct Tape Handy"

When I was directing a child care center, one of the indispensable tools in my director's tool box (the bottom drawer of my desk) was a roll of duct tape.  It seemed like I was always using it to mend a toy, fix a broken screen, or patch a leak in the water table.  One afternoon, in a playful mood I walked into a staff meeting with a piece of duct tape over my mouth. The group burst into

I t is the province of knowledge to speak, and it is the privilege of wisdom to listen.

*Oliver Wendell Holmes*

laughter when one of the teachers said jokingly, "Great, maybe now I'll be able to finish a sentence!" Always one to use self-effacing humor, I peeled the duct tape off and grimaced and said "Ouch!"

That teacher's playful ribbing stung because I knew there was more than a grain of truth to her comment. Listening was not my strong suit. In my fast-paced and spirited style, I would regularly chime in with a response before a teacher finished saying what she or he wanted to say. Over the years I've worked diligently on becoming a better listener. Now when I am tempted to interrupt or finish someone's sentence, I metaphorically grab for my duct tape and put it over my mouth. Works wonders!

Most directors define *effective communication* as the ability to deliver a clear message. Few define it as the sharing of information. The most effective leaders I know have shifted thinking about communication as "articulating a clear message" to "learning and building rapport." They see conversations as an opportunity not for persuading, but rather for building mutual regard and increasing their understanding of another person's point of view. This view changes the whole dynamic of a conversation.

Many leaders assume their job is to solve problems—to give advice and make things better for their staff. Our society reinforces this expectation. In our culture we assume it is our job to fix each other. But when teachers have a problem or when something upsets them, all they may need is someone who cares enough to just listen to them. They don't need advice ("Here's what I would do if I were in your shoes"). They don't need a book or an article on the subject or discussion about the results of recent research in an effort to enlighten them. They just need someone who cares enough to listen. Deep listening is the ultimate expression of caring. It is one of the most treasured gifts you as a leader can offer.

Listening is more than hearing. Intellectually, you are interpreting what you hear and searching for meaning in the nuances of words. Good listening requires empathy, the capacity to see and feel what the speaker sees and feels. It is hard work that involves concentration and emotional sensitivity; but it is essential for achieving interpersonal rapport.

Think about the worst listener you know. What are the things that person does or says that annoy you? Do you share any of these annoying habits? Are there areas you could improve in your listening skills? Read the statements in Exercise 9 and consider what changes you might make in your listening style to enhance your leadership capacity.

❑ I usually think about my response while the other person is talking.

❑ I am impatient with people who don't get right to the point.

❑ I often finish sentences for other people.

❑ I am too busy to engage in friendly chit chat.

❑ I carry on a conversation with someone while I am doing another task (sorting papers, organizing my desk, doodling).

❑ Sometimes I just "tune out" when the topic of conversation doesn't interest me.

❑ When I know what the other person is trying to say, I interrupt and respond.

❑ Sometimes I am so busy focusing on the details of what someone says, I miss their main point.

❑ I find it difficult to maintain eye contact while another person is talking, so I tend to look at other objects in the room.

❑ I am inclined to give answers and solutions when staff approach me about issues.

❑ I feel uncomfortable when people express anger, hurt, discouragement, or hopelessness, so I try to say things that will make the feelings go away.

❑ I occasionally sneak a look at my watch while others are talking to me.

❑ I find myself debating issues with people rather than discussing them.

❑ I often interrupt a speaker to ask questions for clarification.

❑ I am uncomfortable with pauses during conversations.

If the person you are talking to doesn't appear to be listening, be patient. It may simply be that he has a small piece of fluff in his ear.

*Winnie the Pooh*

## "The Whole is Greater Than the Sum of Its Parts"

When I was a child I visited a friend of the family who lived in one of those "ready-to-assemble" houses ordered from the Sears, Roebuck and Company catalog. It was amazing. Every component needed—lumber, window frames, paint and varnish, side paneling, nuts and bolts—had been shipped by rail along with a detailed blueprint for putting the house together. For the families who ordered these ready-to-assemble kits, the 30,000 pieces spread out on their property were shaped into something truly significant—a home.

There are numerous examples in daily life of the whole being greater than the sum of its parts. Think of the last time you attended a concert. Each section of an orchestra produces music, but how much more powerful is the music when all parts—strings, woodwinds, percussion, brass—work together. Or think of a major event you've been involved in, such as a fundraiser or a theatrical production, in which the efforts of individuals working on their separate parts created a kind of synergy so the final result was something far greater than the individual contributions.

In his short and entertaining book *Sacred Hoops*, basketball coach Phil Jackson shares his personal philosophy and hard-earned lessons that certainly speak to the wisdom of this bumper sticker. "Most leaders," says Jackson, "tend to view teamwork as a social engineering problem: take X group, add Y motivational technique, and get Z results. But working with the Bulls I've learned that the most effective way to forge a winning team is to call on the players' need to connect with something larger than themselves. Even for those who don't consider themselves 'spiritual' in a conventional sense, creating a successful team—whether it's an NBA champion or a record-setting sales force—is essentially a spiritual act. It requires the individuals involved to surrender their self-interest for the greater good so that the whole adds up to more than the sum of its parts." With several NBA championships under his belt, Jackson surely understands the concept of synergy.

How do effective directors go about nurturing the norms of collaboration that make synergistic work relationships possible? They emphasize cooperative goals, encourage the exchange and sharing of professional resources, and use the terminology of interdependence whenever possible. Most important, they regularly ask teachers about their perceptions of how the staff functions. Appendix C, a Collaboration Questionnaire, is an assessment tool you can use for this purpose. The aggregate data will give you some ideas on ways you can promote synergy in your work setting.

The power of the We is stronger than the power of Me.

*Phil Jackson*

## "It's the Little Things"

After a routine biopsy a few years ago, I heard those three dreaded words that one hopes never to hear. I sat stunned as my doctor told me about the rare form of salivary gland cancer that had been detected. After learning about my options, I asked him to recommend some articles and books I could read to better understand the physiology of my body and the disease that had invaded it. He turned to me and in a dismissive tone said, "I wouldn't recommend that. A little knowledge is a dangerous thing." I left that doctor's office as upset with his flippant remark as I was with my diagnosis.

A few months later, while reading a news magazine, I came across an interesting tidbit of information. Physicians who have more malpractice claims are perceived by their patients as poor communicators, unavailable, rushed, and insensitive. Those who have virtually no malpractice claims are perceived as available, thorough, sensitive, and willing to answer questions fully. Judging from my own emotional reaction to one doctor, I fully understood why.

Humans share a universal longing to be valued; to be considered as significant. So deep is the need to feel significant that it virtually regulates all of our key decisions in life—choice of career, selection of partner, general lifestyle. Effective leaders understand the power of this drive and their role in crafting work environments that contribute to each employee's sense of purpose and self-esteem. Our self-esteem, after all, is our most prized possession.

It is not surprising that teachers' perception of how they are valued at work is a prime predictor of staff turnover. The less significant people feel in their work setting, the less likely they are to stick around. Many well-intentioned people go into teaching but leave after a few short years. True, low salaries and benefits may contribute to their decision, but many leave because they simply don't feel honored. A person's loyalty to the center is in large part a function of how he or she feels appreciated.

It isn't the dramatic gestures—the year-end staff party at a fancy restaurant—that makes people feel significant. It's the little things each day, every day, that contribute to a heightened sense of self-esteem. The little things may not cost a penny, but they do take time. They require genuine acts of caring. They require conscious and deliberate thought about ways to lift people's spirits and make them feel important. Here are some of the little things you can do to make staff feel they are valued:

- Always acknowledge staff using their names, "Good morning, Olivia." "Thank you, Derek." "How thoughtful of you, Jana."
- Take time to learn about their personal lives—a son's ear infection, the dog's escape from the kennel, the latest home remodeling disaster.

People don't care how much you know until they know how much you care.

*John Maxwell*

Treat your teachers as you would have them treat children.

*Margie Carter*

- Pay attention to their likes and dislikes. This will help you personalize your acknowledgements so they are more meaningful.
- Get to know people's hopes and dreams.
- Give them their own business cards.
- Learn the key phrases and familiar expressions of their home language.
- Be flexible when people have personal crises.
- Let them know their opinion counts.
- Get back to them promptly.
- Stay attuned to staff members' needs, both for resources and for professional growth.
- Show your appreciation by putting short personal notes or happy grams in their mailboxes.
- Do everything in your power to make sure staff experience success most of the day.

## "Laughter Is the Shortest Distance Between Two People"

It has been said that the average four-year-old laughs 400 or more times a day, but the average 40-year-old only laughs 15 times a day. I can't imagine these data actually came from a tightly controlled empirical study, but the idea that we lose our sense of humor as we grow older is certainly an interesting one. Is it that we so tired and overwhelmed by the serious demands of adulthood that we can't keep up with those preschoolers?

If I had to think of an instant barometer to evaluate the overall climate of an early childhood program, it would be the "laughter factor"—the amount of spontaneous, light-hearted laughter that fills the air. Kids and adults don't laugh when they are under stress or when tension is high (unless of course it's a nervous, anxious laugh). True laughter can only happen when people feel good—free and open to express themselves through humor.

The work of caring for and educating young children is indeed a serious enterprise, but that doesn't mean we can't infuse levity into our workplace. We know that laughter is a wonderful bonding experience between kids. The same holds true for adults. We spend more time at work than at any other activity we do, so why shouldn't we make our work settings fun-filled places to spend time?

In his book *Anatomy of an Illness*, Norman Cousins talks about the healing effects of laughter and the physiological and biochemical changes that take place in the brain when laughter occurs. There are now certified laughter leaders who conduct seminars about the healing effects of laughter and a worldwide network of laughter clubs to teach folks how to increase the laughter quotient in their lives.

They say enthusiasm is contagious, and so is the lack of it.  If you've ever flown Southwest Airlines, you know how the spontaneous (and often irreverent) humor of the flight crew creates a playful and entertaining experience for the passengers.  Just like norms of caring and sharing, norms of laughter have to be cultivated. So add *laughter specialist* to the other skills in your leadership basket.  I heard that Debbie Fields asks new recruits to her cookie empire to sing "Happy Birthday to You" during their job interview.  Ms. Fields is clearly someone who wants employees who shine in the customer service area.  Perhaps your early childhood program isn't so different.

Assess how laughter is (or isn't) an integral part of the life of your center. Review the times you and your staff laughed in the past week.  I mean *really* laughed.  Have you created the climate where fun is encouraged, where spontaneous moments of humor are celebrated?  If you are serious about injecting some humor into your workplace, here are a few things you might try:

- Designate one bulletin board as a place to post cartoons, jokes, and humorous photos (maybe in the bathroom).
- Attach a cartoon or a short joke to the memos you distribute.
- Institute Crazy Hairdo Day, an Ugly Sweater Day, or an Outrageous Outfit Day. Award joke prizes for winners.
- Host a pajama party where all children and teachers wear their pajamas.
- Keep a camera handy and take candid shots of teachers and children. Post these photos on your humor board.
- Use fun props like Slinky toys, Koosh Balls, or Silly Putty during staff meetings to add a bit of levity to discussions.
- Find reasons to celebrate.  Create fun rituals and traditions that bring smiles to people's faces.

## "Dedication Doesn't Have to Mean Deadication"

Being an administrator of an early childhood program is not just a state of employment; it is a state of mind.  So many individuals who don the director's hat with noble intentions of creating exemplary centers end up leaving the field frustrated, depleted, and disillusioned. They burn out.  They find that there is simply too much to do and too many people tugging on their sleeve for help, advice, and support.  Are you at risk of burning out?  Ask yourself these questions:

- Do you dread leaving your center for a long weekend or a short vacation because of the mountain of work that will pile up in your absence?
- Do you feel you do the work of several people and many things not in line with your job description?
- Does your work consume your whole life, rarely allowing you time to pursue outside interests?

PEANUTS reprinted by permission of United Feature Syndicate. Inc.

If you answered affirmatively to these three questions, you may be at risk of becoming another burnout statistic; a member of the Director-Has-Been Club. The irony from a mental health perspective is that while many directors express concern that they cannot continue to perform their jobs at their current level of intensity, they feel helpless in knowing how to modify their jobs to be more manageable. The frustrations that directors experience are not inconsequential.

A common theme expressed by many directors is that they are expected to be all things to all people. Women in particular often define themselves as moral agents in terms of their capacity to care. Their sense of self-worth is tied to how much they give to others. The result of this orientation is that many women put their own needs at the bottom of the list after children, staff, and family members—even to the point of depletion. Diane, a preschool director, captures this feeling poignantly when she uses the metaphor of an ATM machine to describe her job. "Just like an ATM machine, I'm always ready to give different amounts of time, energy, and care to different people at a moment's notice."

How do you structure a job so that your own needs are met? Psychologists use the term *affective neutrality* to describe the capacity to balance compassion with emotional detachment. This is the key to becoming a long-term thriver in the field—the ability to emotionally close the door at the end of the day. Everyone deserves and needs time for renewing body and spirit. Those who have no fire in themselves cannot warm others.

Individuals in control of their lives have a deliberate game plan. They are well informed, sensitive to the stress indicators in their own behavior, and realistic in assessing their skills and resources. They have learned to put their jobs in perspective by adding diversity and interest to their lives. In other words, people who thrive in early childhood education do not do so by happenstance. Their actions declare that they are not passive about their destiny, not controlled by events. Rather, they are social engineers shaping their environment to meet their needs. Here are just a few things that you can do:

I have the right to do less than what is humanly possible

*Erma Bombeck*

- Learn to say no with sensitive assertiveness.

- Diversify your interests. Don't define who you are solely by your professional accomplishments.

- Give up on the idea that more is better.

- Observe what gives you energy and what drains you. Tune into your natural rhythms to maximize your energy potential.

- Seek and ask for support. Don't wait for it to be offered.

## "You Can't Please All the People All the Time"

You may have picked up this book because you wanted to know how to become the director staff *all* want to work for. Well, let's dispel that myth right now. You can't please all the people all the time. No matter how hard you try, you will always disappoint some people some of the time; and that is okay.

You'll always have parents who want you to change the program to be more academic and others that want you to lighten up and allow more unstructured play time. You'll always have teachers who have personal issues they'd like you to help resolve. And you'll always have professional colleagues who want you to serve on a committee or volunteer for a project.

The teachers and support staff you work with on a day-to-day basis, the board or agency executive to whom you report, the parents you serve, and the professional colleagues you work with in your community all have grand expectations for you—some of them realistic, and some of them not. Part of becoming an effective leader is accepting that you will never be able to win the approval of everyone you work with. There will always be someone eager to tell you how you could do your job differently (better) or use your time more wisely (to meet their agenda).

As blasphemous as it may sound, one of the best ways to become a more effective leader is to *lower your expectations*. Especially for perfectionists and high achievers, this may be the only prescription that really works. Destructive stress can result from setting unrealistic expectations. How about becoming the director that 80 percent of the people want to work for 80 percent of the time!

Joking aside, the key point of this last bumper sticker is to encourage you to thicken that outer layer of skin. Take in the unsolicited advice, friendly suggestions, and stinging criticisms that come your way. Weigh them against your core values, and then decide what is best for you to do given the time, resources, and personal energy available. This will help you be true to yourself and comfortable with the knowledge that you can never please all the people all the time.

**CHAPTER 6**

# What Does it Mean to Walk the Talk?

As director, you are the CEO—the Chief Example for Others. You are in the spotlight, whether you like it or not. Every decision you make and every action you take is noticed, scrutinized, and evaluated. You are on stage even when the door to your office is closed.

In this chapter we'll explore what it means to *walk the talk*. How do you become a leader of integrity, living your personal code of ethics every day on the job? We'll also look at the issue of leadership succession; how do you ensure that your program stays strong and healthy after you've turned over keys and moved on?

## Striving for Authenticity

Directors who walk the talk practice what they preach. Their actions are consistent with what they say. In other words, they are authentic leaders. They don't change their behavior depending on who is in the room or who might be listening at the moment. Imagine how you would talk and behave if you knew your telephone was bugged or your every move being captured on videotape.

Being authentic means leading in a way that is natural for you and not trying to be someone else. It means regularly appraising your strengths and weaknesses. The more aware you are of yourself, the better you will be able to develop a team that reflects complementary strengths, adding value to your organization.

Being an authentic leader doesn't mean you have to have all the answers or that somehow you need to be a paragon of perfection. To the contrary, the best (and ironically the most confident) leaders are those who are willing to let others know they are works in progress—that every day they think about how they can improve their leadership skills to better serve others. What a powerful role model you can be for your staff if you can demonstrate by your own example that self development is a lifelong journey regardless of where you are in the organizational tower of power.

There is another word that captures the essence of authentic leadership. It is *integrity*. When we refer to someone as "a person of integrity," what we really mean is that person shows a consistency between personal beliefs and actions. Integrity can be viewed as a set of principles you hold yourself accountable to and demonstrate in your daily behavior toward others. Some say that integrity is your character in action.

E xample isn't the best way to influence others—it's the only way

*Albert Schweitzer*

It is unfortunate that most people work harder on their image than on their integrity. Image is what we want people think about us. Integrity is who we really are. Ask yourself these questions to get a clearer sense of how you demonstrate your personal integrity:

- Are you known for honoring your promises and commitments?
- Have you done all you can to build trusting relationships with your colleagues?
- Do you hold yourself to the same standards you hold others?
- Do you exhibit a positive attitude about your work?
- Do you assign blame or find fault in others just to bolster your own ego?
- Do your employees believe you deliver on your promises?
- Are you the same person no matter whom you are with?
- Do you make decisions based on what is best for others or what is best for yourself?
- Do you recognize others for their efforts and contributions to your success?

### What Does It Take to Walk the Talk?

- The ability to accept people as they are, not as you would like them to be

- The ability to approach relationships and problems in terms of the present rather than the past

- The ability to treat those who are close to you with the same courteous attention that you would extend to strangers and casual acquaintances

- The ability to trust others, even if the risk seems great

- The ability to do without constant approval and recognition from others

*Adapted from Arbuckle, M., & Murray, L. (1989). Building systems for professional growth. Andover, MA: The Maine Department of Educational and Cultural Services.*

Remember, you become what you practice most. You can choose to be ...

- a leader who is caring, compassionate, kind, and humble
- a leader who contributes to, learns from, and influences the learning of others
- a leader who works to instill leadership capacity at all levels of the organization
- a leader of integrity

or not.

## Living Your Personal Code of Ethics

As individuals, we each have a personal perspective on the difference between right and wrong, between good and bad. Our sense of ethics—our personal code of conduct—comes from our core values and beliefs. Consciously or unconsciously, this code is what controls our actions and serves as our moral compass.

Administering an early childhood program is all about ethics. It is about the choices you make every day about how you use the power and influence inherent in your leadership position, how you treat other people, and how you conduct the business aspects of your center's operation.

We rely on laws to define the black and white issues involved in professional practice. For example, we have federal laws regulating hiring and firing employees, state licensing standards defining group size and ratios, and city building and sanitation codes regulating health and safety issues. But we rely on our own personal code of ethics to make the tough judgment calls, those difficult decisions that fall in the gray zone of leadership.

Given the spotlight on corporate corruption over the past few years, one might easily conclude that in America, *business ethics* is an oxymoron. We have too few models of moral leaders acting with high ethical principles. That's why your role as a leader in your organization is so crucial. The ethical climate you set influences the actions and behavior of all those around you.

Take a moment now to reflect on your own behavior as you complete the ethics self-assessment in Exercise 10 on page 86.

W hat we are communicates far more eloquently than anything we say or do.

*Stephen Covey*

*During the last several months, have I...*

❏ conducted personal business on the center's time?

❏ used or taken resources from the center for personal use?

❏ made exceptions to the stated policies of the center for myself?

❏ called in sick when I wasn't?

❏ changed my demeanor or behavior in front of parents or board members?

❏ used a derogatory term when referring to another individual or ethnic group?

❏ engaged in negative gossip?

❏ snooped into a co-worker's conversations or private affairs?

❏ passed along information that was shared with me in confidence?

❏ knowingly ignored (or violated) an organizational rule or procedure?

❏ failed to follow through on something I said I would do?

❏ withheld information others needed?

❏  fudged on a time sheet, expense voucher, or report?

❏ exaggerated the truth so others would think more highly of me?

❏ taken or accepted credit for something someone else did?

❏ failed to admit to or correct a mistake I made?

The time is always right to do what is right.

*Martin Luther King Jr.*

Adapted from Harvey, E., & Airitam, S. (2002). *Ethics 4 everyone*. Dallas, TX: Performance Systems Corporation.

If you found yourself checking any of the items in this exercise, what excuses and rationalizations did you use to justify your actions?

- Everyone else does it.
- They'll never miss it.
- Nobody really cares anyway.
- My supervisor does it.
- No one will know.
- Some rules are meant to be broken.

E thics is always 'an inside-out proposition' involving free will.

*Al Gini*

---

## Before You Act, Ask Yourself . . .

✓ Is it legal?

✓ Does it comply with our center's rules and guidelines?

✓ Is it in sync with our organizational values?

✓ Does this behavior fit with my view of myself at my best?

✓ Will I feel guilt-free if I do it?

✓ Would I be comfortable if my supervisor (board, parents) knew about this?

✓ Does it match our center's stated commitments and guarantees?

✓ Would I do it to my family or best friends?

✓ Would I be perfectly okay with someone doing it to me?

✓ What would the person I admire the most do in this situation?

Adapted from Harvey, E., & Airitam, S. (2002). *Ethics 4 everyone*. Dallas, TX: Performance Systems Corporation.

---

Ethics can be described as obedience to the unenforceable. It is the study of right and wrong, duties and obligations. Our profession's code of ethics, developed by the National Association for the Education of Young Children (NAEYC), articulates and affirms the values, beliefs, and purposes of the early childhood practitioners. Ethical conduct is thus defined as conforming to the accepted professional standards of our profession.

Most directors can sort out the right versus the wrong choices. The challenge arises when you are faced with two good choices. What should you do? An ethical dilemma is a situation with no obvious answer; one that requires you to choose between two equally balanced alternatives. It presents a predicament that defies a quick and easy solution, where there is more than one morally justifiable solution.

*Burnece is the owner/director of a small private proprietary center in a mid-size city in the Midwest. She has struggled to keep her center financially strong over the past decade as the economy in her area has ebbed and flowed. A few years ago when there was a dip in the enrollment, she even reduced her own salary by one-half so that she would not have to lay off any of her valued teachers.*

*A fellow director in her town who also operates a for-profit center has asked Burnece to join her in a letter-writing campaign to protest a legislative push in the state to increase the minimum wage. This action is seen by many who run small child care businesses as creating an unfair economic hardship. This situation presents an ethical dilemma for Burnece. A small mandated increase in the minimum wage would have serious repercussions on the financial health of her center. She knows she could not pass on this increase to parents in increased tuition without jeopardizing her enrollment margins. The situation is an ethical dilemma because Burnece feels equally strongly about the need to increase the professionalism and status of the early childhood workforce. She knows that higher salaries and better benefits are one way to accomplish that.*

The situation described in the preceding vignette is typical of many that confront directors of early care and education programs. In such situations when a clear-cut choice is not readily apparent, you need to decide which choice is "more right"—more in line with laws, regulations, your center's mission, and internal policies and procedures. You can also ask yourself which alternative provides the greatest benefit for the largest number of stakeholders; and which alternative sets the best precedent for guiding similar decisions in the future.

## Thinking About Your Successor

Ever wonder what would happen to your center if you were struck by lightening and died? A morbid thought to be sure, but one that makes every director I've posed this question to stand up straight and ponder. Does anyone else on your staff know the password to your computer? Does anyone else on your staff know the combination to the center's safe deposit box? Would anyone on your staff have the range of skills, knowledge, interest, or desire to step into your shoes and fill the leadership void created by your untimely demise?

I posed this hypothetical struck-by-lightening question to 400 directors recently in a survey about leadership succession. The results were amazing. Only 30 percent of the directors were confident that the operation of their center would continue smoothly; that personnel and systems were in place to ensure an efficient transition. Ten percent of the directors responded that chaos would reign if they died suddenly; that no one was equipped to step into their position and assume the leadership role. The remaining directors indicated that things would be shaky but still functional; that someone could cover their responsibilities until a formal search to find a replacement was concluded.

**What is leadership succession?** When you board an airplane, one of the first instructions the flight attendant gives is to think about your exit strategy in case of an emergency. Good advice also for directors of child care programs. A well-crafted risk management plan can help minimize the disastrous consequences to your center should a tragedy befall you. A risk management plan ensures that policies are in place for things like computer passwords and safe deposit box combinations. But a center needs much more than a risk management plan. It also needs a comprehensive leadership succession plan.

The transition of the directorship reverberates throughout a center. It is a significant and pivotal event in the life of an early childhood organization. When done right, it can infuse vitality into a program, providing fresh ideas and new perspectives for the future. When done wrong, it can result in earthquake-like tremors throughout a center, creating instability, uncertainty, and havoc. The replacement of leadership is disruptive because it changes lines of communication, affects decision making, and generally disturbs the equilibrium of daily activities.

Leadership succession planning rests on the supposition that transitions work best when they are approached intentionally. A leadership succession plan is a deliberate and systematic effort by your organization to ensure leadership continuity in the directorship and other key leadership roles. It can help your center develop and retain its most capable employees, preserve your program's institutional memory, and ensure that your organization continues to meet all its legal obligations. Developing a comprehensive leadership succession plan involves thinking about two things: systems and people.

**Are systems in place to ensure a smooth transition?** Assuming you plan a less dramatic departure from Mother Earth than being hit by a bolt of lightening, thinking about leadership succession involves thinking about the infrastructure of your program. Your infrastructure is all the formal and informal systems you have established to ensure that a new replacement can be socialized into your role with a minimum of disruption.

The brightest business people recognize that while death is unavoidable, their organization need not follow them to the grave.

*David Baron*

There is no single formula for managing transitions because each organization is different. If you are an owner of a center and operate a private proprietary program, your needs and interests will be quite different from those of a director of a nonprofit center who is accountable to a governing board or agency executive team. The important point is that regardless of the legal auspice of your program, systems need to be in place to handle both anticipated and unanticipated changes in leadership.

**Are people in place to ensure a smooth transition?** In my research, I have found that only 27 percent of directors feel they were well prepared to handle the range of tasks required of them when they first assumed their administrative roles. This is not surprising given that most directors are promoted into the administrative ranks from teaching. Their classroom experience simply does not prepare them for leading and managing others.

This does not need to be the case. When programs develop a culture of professional development whereby leadership is delegated at all levels of the organization, it is possible to create a center that does not experience chaos when the director leaves. When an administrative position opens, staff have been groomed to move into higher levels of leadership responsibility.

In programs like this, directors think deliberately about job descriptions and create a career lattice within their centers where roles reflect expanding spheres of leadership accountability. In these centers leadership is talked about, practiced, and nurtured at all levels of the organization. Assistant teachers, teachers, support staff, and administrative staff are all given opportunities to develop the technical and interpersonal skills essential for leadership. It is possible, for example, to think about accountability as moving from managing oneself to managing a few others, to managing groups, to managing external constituencies.

Creating a culture of professional development that supports leadership succession also means thinking deliberately about formal and informal mentor relationships. Most leaders in organizations have emerged as leaders because they were identified and mentored by established leaders. Mentors make it safe for fledgling leaders to spread their wings, take on challenging assignments that broaden their knowledge base, and try out new tasks that expand their repertoire of skills.

Take some time to think about what leadership succession means in your center. What are you doing today that will help ensure a smooth transition for your successor, whether you anticipate that transition taking place tomorrow, next year, or ten years from now? A well-crafted succession plan is the best gift you can give your center as a leader who walks the talk.

I t takes a leader to raise up a leader.

*John Maxwell*

## How Directors Build and Sustain Leadership Capacity

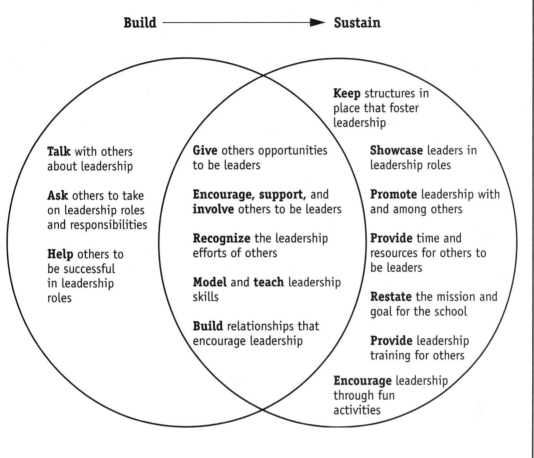

Build ——————▶ Sustain

**Talk** with others about leadership

**Ask** others to take on leadership roles and responsibilities

**Help** others to be successful in leadership roles

**Give** others opportunities to be leaders

**Encourage, support,** and **involve** others to be leaders

**Recognize** the leadership efforts of others

**Model** and **teach** leadership skills

**Build** relationships that encourage leadership

**Keep** structures in place that foster leadership

**Showcase** leaders in leadership roles

**Promote** leadership with and among others

**Provide** time and resources for others to be leaders

**Restate** the mission and goal for the school

**Provide** leadership training for others

**Encourage** leadership through fun activities

# CHAPTER 7

# A Final Word

The concept of zoom provides a wonderful metaphor for the flexibility of effective leadership. Similar to the zoom lens of a camera, leaders must be able to shift from one perspective to another, viewing the same situation from different vantage points when making decisions, building systems, mentoring colleagues, evaluating actions, and serving as agents of change. This means having the capacity to step back and look at the big picture to determine the impact of different actions, while simultaneously being cognizant of the small details that influence people's reactions to any event.

Being able to look at the big picture and focus on the details is an example of one of the many paradoxes inherent in early childhood leadership. A paradox is a statement that appears to be contradictory but is nonetheless true. Here are a few more paradoxes that you'll readily identify with in your work as a leader:

- Promote team effort **and** encourage individual autonomy.
- Involve people **and** make decisions swiftly.
- Be thorough **and** keep it simple.
- Promote change **and** maintain continuity.
- Plan for the future **and** be open to new opportunities.
- Encourage goal consensus **and** diversity of opinion.
- Promote equity **and** make exceptions.
- Keep the ball rolling **and** take time for reflection.

Paradoxes help illustrate the dynamic tensions that define our work. Paradoxes are disconcerting to most people; they tempt us into either/or thinking, asking us to choose between two equally compelling alternatives. Our culture reinforces this orientation with right/wrong, good/bad, appropriate/inappropriate frames for evaluating our choices.

In the end, effective leadership is often about achieving a sense of balance between competing interests. It is about learning to approach the opposites inherent in your work in such a way that they do not cancel each other but rather create new energy from their points of polarity. Effective leadership is about embracing the paradoxes.

Truth is a paradoxical joining of apparent opposites, and if we want to know that truth, we must learn to embrace those opposites as one.

*Parker Palmer*

# For Further Reading

Baldwin, S. (2002). *The playful adult: 500 ways to lighten your spirit and tickle your soul*. Stillwater, MN: Insights.

Baron, D. (1999). *Moses on management*. New York: Pocket Books.

Blanchard, K. (1999). *The heart of a leader*. Tulsa, OK: Honor Books.

Blanchard, K., & Bowles, S. (1998). *Gung Ho!* New York: William Morrow.

Bloom, P.J. (2002). *Making the most of meetings: A practical guide*. Lake Forest, IL: New Horizons.

Bloom, P.J. (2000). *Circle of influence: Implementing shared decision making and participative management*. Lake Forest, IL: New Horizons.

Bloom, P.J. (1992, Spring). The child care center director: A critical determinant of program quality. *Educational Horizons, 70*, 138-145.

Bloom, P.J., & Sheerer, M. (1992). The effect of leadership training on child care program quality. *Early Childhood Research Quarterly, 7*(4), 579-594.

Bloom, P.J., Sheerer, M., & Britz, J. (1991). *Blueprint for action: Achieving center-based change through staff development*. Lake Forest, IL: New Horizons.

Bolman, L., & Deal, T. (2001). *Leading with soul: An uncommon journey of spirit*. San Francisco: Jossey-Bass.

Buckingham, M., & Clifton, D. (2001). *Now, discover your strengths*. New York: The Free Press.

Carlson, R. (1997). *Don't sweat the small stuff... and it's all small stuff*. New York: Hyperion.

Carter, M., & Curtis, D. (1998). *Visionary director: A handbook for dreaming, organizing, and improvising in your center*. St. Paul, MN: Redleaf Press.

Collins, J. (2001). *Good to great: Why some companies make the leap ... and others don't*. New York: HarperCollins.

Culkin, M. L. (Ed.). (2000). *Managing quality in young children's programs: The leader's role*. New York: Teachers College Press.

Covey, S. (1991). *Principle-centered leadership*. New York: Fireside Books.

DePree, M. (1997). *Leading without power*. San Francisco: Jossey-Bass.

Deal, T., & Peterson, K., (1999). *Shaping school culture: The heart of leadership.* San Francisco: Jossey-Bass.

Edelman, M.W. (1999). *Lanterns: A memoir of mentors.* Boston, MA: Beacon Press.

Edwards, M., & Ewen, A. (1996). *360° feedback.* New York: AMACOM.

Feeney, S., & Freeman, N. (2001, May). Ethics and the center director. *Child Care Information Exchange,* 22-25.

Finzel, H. (2000). *The top ten mistakes leaders make.* Colorado Springs,CO: Cook Communications

French, R.P., & Raven, B.H. (1968). Bases of social power. In D. Cartwright and A. Zander (Eds.), *Group dynamics: Research and theory* (pp. 259-270). New York: Harper & Row.

Gardner, J. (1989). The tasks of leadership. In W. Rosenbach and R. Taylor (Eds.), *Contemporary issues in leadership* (pp. 24-33). Boulder, CO: Westview Press.

Gardner, H. (2001). *Good work: When excellence and ethics meet.* New York: Basic Books.

Gelatt, H.B. (1991). *Creative decision making: Using positive uncertainty.* Menlo Park, CA: Crisp.

Goleman, D., Boyatzis, R., & McKee A. (2002). *Primal leadership: Realizing the power of emotional intelligence.* Boston: MA: Harvard Business School Press.

Harvey, E., & Airitam, S. (2002). *Ethics 4 everyone: The handbook for integrity-based business practices.* Dallas, TX: The Walk the Talk Company.

Helgesen, S. (1990). *The female advantage: Women's ways of leadership.* New York: Doubleday.

Hoy, W., & Miskel, C. (2001). *Educational administration: Theory, research, and practice* (6th ed.). New York: Random House.

Huseman, R., & Hatfield, J. (1989). *Managing the equity factor.* Boston: Houghton Mifflin.

Jensen, B. (2000). *Simplicity: The new competitive advantage in a world of more, better, faster.* Cambridge, MA: Perseus Books.

Johnson, S. (1998). *Who moved my cheese?* New York: G.P. Putnam's Sons.

Jones, L. B. (1995). *Jesus CEO*. New York: Hyperion.

Jude-York, D., & Wise, S. (1997). *Multipoint feedback: A 360° catalyst for change.* Menlo Park, CA; Crisp.

Kagan, S. L., & Bowman, B. (Eds.). (1997). *Leadership in early care and education.* Washington, DC: National Association for the Education of Young Children.

Kegan, R., & Lahey, L. L. (2001). *How the way we talk can change the way we work: Seven languages for transformation.* San Francisco: Jossey-Bass.

Kouzes, J., & Posner, B. (2002). *Leadership challenge.* San Francisco: Jossey-Bass.

Lambert, L. (2003). *Leadership capacity for lasting school improvement.* Alexandria, VA: Association for Supervision and Curriculum Development.

Leithwood, K. (1992, February). The move toward transformational leadership. *Educational Leadership,* 8-12.

Lundin, S., Paul, H., & Christensen, J. (2000). *Fish!* New York: Hyperion.

McGregor, D. (1960). *The human side of enterprise.* New York: McGraw-Hill.

Mackay, H. (1996). *Swim with the sharks.* New York: Fawcett Books.

Maxwell, J. (2000). *Developing the leader within you.* Nashville, TN: Thomas Nelson.

Mohr, N., & Dichter, A. (2001, June). Building a learning organization. *Phi Delta Kappan,* 744-47.

Neugebauer, B., & Neugebauer, R. (Eds.). (1998). *The art of leadership: Managing early childhood organizations.* Redmond, WA: Exchange Press.

O'Connor, S.D. (2003). *The majesty of the law: Reflections of a Supreme Court Justice.* New York: Random House.

Palmer, P. (1998). *The courage to teach.* San Francisco: Jossey-Bass.

Project Zero. (2001). *Making learning visible.* Cambridge, MA: Project Zero, Harvard University.

Renz, D.O. (2003, Summer). *Developing leadership in the new millennium: Building capacity in the early care and education community.* Kansas City, MO: Midwest Center for Nonprofit Leadership at the University of Missouri-Kansas City.

Rodd, J. (1994). *Leadership in early childhood: The pathway to professionalism.* New York: Teachers College Press.

Schwarz, R. (2002). *The skilled facilitator: A comprehensive resource for consultants, facilitators, managers, trainers, and coaches.* San Francisco: Jossey-Bass.

Sciarra, D.J., & Dorsey, A.G. (2002). *Leaders and supervisors in child care programs.* Albany, NY: Delmar.

Schmuck, R.A., & Runkel, P.J. (1985). *The handbook of organization development in schools.* Palo Alto, CA: Mayfield Publishing.

Spears, L.C. (Ed.). (1998). *Insights on leadership: Service, stewardship, spirit, and servant-leadership.* New York: John Wiley & Sons.

Wolfred, T. (2002, Winter). Stepping up: A board's challenge in leadership transition. *The Nonprofit Quarterly, 9*(4), 18-23.

Zeece, P. D. (1998). Power lines—The use and abuse of power in child care programming. In B. Neugebauer & R. Neugebauer (Eds.), *The art of leadership: Managing early childhood organizations* (pp. 29-33). Redmond, WA: Exchange Press.

# Appendices

**A.** Beliefs and Values Questionnaire

**B.** Multi-Rater Leadership Assessment

**C.** Collaboration Questionnaire

## Beliefs and Values Questionnaire

### Rationale:
Teachers' attitudes and beliefs about children provide the foundation for their philosophy of teaching. Because beliefs are grounded in one's values, they have a strong impact on shaping an individual's behavior. Teachers' values govern how they react when confronted with the ethical dilemmas that occur from time to time. The director's role is to ensure that the beliefs and values of individual teachers are consonant with the shared beliefs and stated philosophy of the center.

This assessment asks teachers to reflect on their attitudes and beliefs about children, parents, and their own teaching role in the classroom. The information gleaned from this assessment will help you better understand your teachers' values and beliefs, which serve as the foundation for their teaching practices.

### Directions:
Explain to staff that there are no right or wrong answers in completing this assessment. The purpose is to gather information regarding their beliefs and values about working with young children. The answers can serve as a springboard for a staff meeting devoted to the topic of teaching beliefs and values. Include in the discussion an opportunity for individuals to share how their responses to some of the questions on this questionnaire may have changed over time.

*From Bloom, P. J., Sheerer, M., & Britz., J. (1991). Blueprint for action: Achieving center-based change through staff development. Lake Forest, IL: New Horizons. (Assessment Tool #18, pp. 232-33). Reprinted with permission.*

# Beliefs and Values

Values are enduring beliefs—ideas that we cherish and regard highly. Values influence the decisions we make and the courses of action we follow. Some values we prize more highly than others; they become standards by which we live. The purpose of this assessment is to provide an opportunity for you to share the values and beliefs that guide your teaching practices.

**PART I.   Complete the following sentences.**

1.  I think children are generally _____

2.  When children are unhappy, it's usually because _____

3.  I get angry when children _____

4.  The most important thing a teacher can do is _____

5.  Children should not _____

6.  All children are_____

7.  I wish parents would _____

8.  When parents _____ I feel _____

**PART II.   Circle the five traits and characteristics you would like children to be or have as a result of their preschool experience with you.**

| | | |
|---|---|---|
| adventurous | appreciation of beauty | determined |
| affectionate | inquisitive | energetic |
| polite | respectful | friendly |
| altruistic | self-starter | obedient |
| caring | sense of humor | spontaneous |
| honest | industrious | persistent |
| assertive | creative | proud |
| confident | independent thinker | risk taker |
| cheerful | desire to excel | open-minded |

From Bloom, P. J., Sheerer, M., & Britz., J. (1991). *Blueprint for action: Achieving center-based change through staff development.* Lake Forest, IL: New Horizons. (Assessment Tool #18, pp. 232-33). Reprinted with permission.

## Multi-Rater Leadership Assessment

**Rationale:**
The leadership style of the director is a critical factor influencing the effectiveness of an early childhood program. The director more than anyone else is responsible for creating a work climate based on mutual respect in which people work together to accomplish shared goals. The success of this endeavor rests in large part on the director's ability to show leadership traits that inspire, motivate, and move people toward a common vision.

Understanding how others interpret and experience your leadership behavior is central to developing a leadership style that supports your shared goals. This assessment provides your staff with an opportunity to evaluate your leadership performance in 25 areas.

**Directions:**
Distribute the two-page *"My Director..."* feedback form and a blank envelope to all employees who work at your center more than ten hours per week. You may also choose to give the form to other individuals (e.g., board members, supervisor, center owner) whom you feel have an important perspective on your performance.

Place a box labeled Survey Return Box in your center's office or staff room, and ask respondents to put their envelopes holding their completed surveys in this box. Reassure individuals about the confidentiality of their responses. Also, be sure to complete the assessment yourself so you can compare your responses with the collective perceptions of others.

## Scoring:

Use the blank summary sheet to record your own scores and those of each rater. (An example of a completed form is located on page 49.)

- Enter your own score for each of the 25 items in the column headed "Self-Rating."

- In the columns under the heading "Other Raters," enter the scores for each individual who completed the "*My Director...*" feedback form.

- For each trait, generate an average score by totaling the respondents' ratings and then dividing the total by the number of respondents. Record the result under the "Average" heading in the far right column. Do this for each of the 25 traits.

- Generate an average rating by each respondent by adding the scores going down each column. (The totals will range from 25-125.) Then divide each total (near the bottom of the form) by 25 (the number of traits).

- Generate an average overall rating for the "Other Raters" by adding the individual average ratings (at the bottom) and dividing by the total by the number of respondents.

## Interpreting the Ratings:

As you compare your own ratings with the average ratings of your colleagues, look for four themes:

- Agreed-upon strengths—traits that both you and your staff rated high.

- Unrealized strengths—traits that you rated low, but your staff rated high.

- Areas for growth—traits that both you and your staff rated low.

- Blind spots—traits that you rated high, but your staff rated low.

# "My Director ..."

Dear Staff:

One of the hallmarks of an effective early childhood professional is the ability to reflect on his or her performance. Your feedback about my leadership style is important in helping me grow professionally. Please take a few minutes to complete this leadership traits evaluation form. When you have finished, insert it in the attached envelope and put it in the Survey Return Box in the office. There is no need for you to put your name on the form.

*Thank you.*

(Your signature)

Circle the numeral from 1 to 5 (1 = strongly disagree, 5 = strongly agree) that most nearly represents your assessment of my performance in each of the areas described.

| *My director is ...* | Strongly disagree | | | | Strongly agree |
|---|---|---|---|---|---|
| **accessible**—is available when staff, parents, or community representatives need to reach him/her. | 1 | 2 | 3 | 4 | 5 |
| **collaborative**—encourages staff to participate in centerwide decisions impacting their welfare. | 1 | 2 | 3 | 4 | 5 |
| **confident**—has a can-do spirit and sense of optimism about the future. | 1 | 2 | 3 | 4 | 5 |
| **creative**—looks for new and novel ways to solve problems and keep things interesting. | 1 | 2 | 3 | 4 | 5 |
| **dependable**—can be counted on to follow through on commitments and responsibilities. | 1 | 2 | 3 | 4 | 5 |
| **direct**—is clear and forthright in both oral and written communication. | 1 | 2 | 3 | 4 | 5 |
| **empathetic**—is genuinely concerned about the well-being of the staff and children. | 1 | 2 | 3 | 4 | 5 |
| **enthusiastic**—has the energy and stamina to handle the daily demands of the director's job. | 1 | 2 | 3 | 4 | 5 |
| **ethical**—demonstrates integrity in both words and actions. | 1 | 2 | 3 | 4 | 5 |
| **fair**—looks at all sides of an issue and takes into consideration equity factors when making tough decisions. | 1 | 2 | 3 | 4 | 5 |
| **flexible**—is willing to make accommodations when necessary to support staff and families. | 1 | 2 | 3 | 4 | 5 |

| | Strongly disagree | | | | Strongly agree |
|---|---|---|---|---|---|
| **friendly**—displays a warm and gracious manner to staff, parents, and visitors to the center. | 1 | 2 | 3 | 4 | 5 |
| **a good listener**—knows how to listen respectfully and attentively to others. | 1 | 2 | 3 | 4 | 5 |
| **inspiring**—has high expectations and helps people achieve their personal best. | 1 | 2 | 3 | 4 | 5 |
| **knowledgeable**—keeps current about new developments and best practices in the field of early childhood education. | 1 | 2 | 3 | 4 | 5 |
| **objective**—makes decisions after seeking different perspectives and weighing the advantages and disadvantages of each. | 1 | 2 | 3 | 4 | 5 |
| **open**—shares important information about the center with staff and parents. | 1 | 2 | 3 | 4 | 5 |
| **optimistic**—has a positive attitude and keeps things in a healthy perspective. | 1 | 2 | 3 | 4 | 5 |
| **organized**—knows how to create organizational systems to ensure the smooth functioning of the program. | 1 | 2 | 3 | 4 | 5 |
| **predictable**—ensures that expectations are clearly defined and policies are consistently enforced. | 1 | 2 | 3 | 4 | 5 |
| **a problem solver**—gathers needed data to solve problems in a systematic and timely manner. | 1 | 2 | 3 | 4 | 5 |
| **resourceful**—knows how to tap community resources to get things done. | 1 | 2 | 3 | 4 | 5 |
| **respectful**—treats each employee as a unique and special person and appreciates diversity as an organizational asset. | 1 | 2 | 3 | 4 | 5 |
| **supportive**—promotes the professional growth of staff by providing opportunities for ongoing training and development. | 1 | 2 | 3 | 4 | 5 |
| **visionary**—has a sense of mission and communicates a clear vision for the future. | 1 | 2 | 3 | 4 | 5 |

What two words or phrases most accurately describe my leadership style?

_____     _____

Bloom, P. J. (2003). *Leadership in Action: How Effective Directors Get Things Done*. Lake Forest, IL: New Horizons.

# Multi-Rater Summary Form

Name: _____

| Trait | Self Rating | Other Raters | | | | | | | | | | Average of other raters |
|---|---|---|---|---|---|---|---|---|---|---|---|---|
| Accessible | | | | | | | | | | | | |
| Collaborative | | | | | | | | | | | | |
| Confident | | | | | | | | | | | | |
| Creative | | | | | | | | | | | | |
| Dependable | | | | | | | | | | | | |
| Direct | | | | | | | | | | | | |
| Empathetic | | | | | | | | | | | | |
| Enthusiastic | | | | | | | | | | | | |
| Ethical | | | | | | | | | | | | |
| Fair | | | | | | | | | | | | |
| Flexible | | | | | | | | | | | | |
| Friendly | | | | | | | | | | | | |
| A good listener | | | | | | | | | | | | |
| Inspiring | | | | | | | | | | | | |
| Knowledgeable | | | | | | | | | | | | |
| Objective | | | | | | | | | | | | |
| Open | | | | | | | | | | | | |
| Optimistic | | | | | | | | | | | | |
| Organized | | | | | | | | | | | | |
| Predictable | | | | | | | | | | | | |
| A problem solver | | | | | | | | | | | | |
| Resourceful | | | | | | | | | | | | |
| Respectful | | | | | | | | | | | | |
| Supportive | | | | | | | | | | | | |
| Visionary | | | | | | | | | | | | |
| | | | | | | | | | | | | |
| **Total** | | | | | | | | | | | | |
| **Average rating** | | | | | | | | | | | | |

Agreed-upon strengths: _____

Unrealized strengths: _____

Areas for growth: _____

Blind spots: _____

## Collaboration Questionnaire

### Rationale:

An esprit de corps, that feeling of sharing and caring for one another, is essential for achieving a high-functioning team. This tool assesses staff's perceptions regarding their overall co-worker relations—specifically, the extent to which they feel teaching at the center is a team effort directed toward the collaborative goal of improving center effectiveness. How well the teachers work together depends in large part on the harmony of their interests within the center—the degree to which they share similar goals and objectives.

### Directions:

Distribute the Collaboration Questionnaire and a blank envelope to all teaching and support staff who work at the center more than ten hours per week. Place a box labeled Questionnaire Return Box in your center's office or staff room and ask staff to put their completed questionnaires in this box.

### Directions:

Since many of the questions on this instrument deal with sensitive social relationship issues, it is wise to have an outside person tabulate the results and summarize the responses to the open-ended question. The scores for this instrument will range from 0 to 10. To determine your center's collaboration index,

    a.  Tally the number of checks next to items 1, 3, 5, 6, 9,    Total _____ (a)

    b.  Tally the number of checks next to items 2, 4, 7, 8, 10    Total _____ (b)

    c.  Individual total score equals (a) - (b) + 5 = _____ (c)

    d.  Add together all the individual scores and divide the sum by the number of staff completing the questionnaire to determine your center's collaboration index.

        A score of 7 to 10 indicates that your staff has quite positive feelings about teamwork at your center. A score lower than 4 indicates there is room for improving the climate of collaboration.

From Bloom, P. J., Sheerer, M., & Britz., J. (1991). *Blueprint for action: Achieving center-based change through staff development*. Lake Forest, IL: New Horizons. *(Assessment Tool #6, pp. 192-93). Reprinted with permission.*

# Collaboration Questionnaire

This questionnaire assesses your perceptions of the degree to which the center's staff functions as a team. Your honest and candid responses to these questions are appreciated. When you have completed your questionnaire, please put it in the envelope provided and place it in the Questionnaire Return Box in the office. It is not necessary for you to include your name.

Put a check (✓) next to those items which accurately reflect how you feel.

_____ 1. Other teachers at the center regularly seek my advice about professional issues and problems.

_____ 2. I don't offer advice to other teachers about their teaching unless they ask me for it.

_____ 3. I regularly share teaching ideas, materials, and resources with other teachers at the center.

_____ 4. I believe that good teaching is a gift; it isn't something you can really learn from anyone else.

_____ 5. If teachers at this center feel that another teacher is not doing a good job, they will exert some pressure on him/her to improve.

_____ 6. The director encourages teachers to plan together and collaborate on instructional units, field trips, and classroom activities.

_____ 7. Substitutes at the center often do not know what our staff is trying to accomplish and what is expected of them.

_____ 8. Most of the time the other teachers in the center don't know what I do in my classroom with my group of children.

_____ 9. I see myself as part of a team and share responsibility for our center's successes and shortcomings.

_____10. I can go for days in our center without talking to anyone about my teaching.

Select the three words that most accurately describe other staff at the center.

| | | | |
|---|---|---|---|
| cooperative | friendly | isolated | cautious |
| competitive | trusting | guarded | helpful |
| caring | cliquish | open | mistrustful |

What suggestions do you have that might increase opportunities for collaboration and teamwork at our center (for example, modifying work schedules, changing the layout of space)?

From Bloom, P. J., Sheerer, M., & Britz., J. (1991). _Blueprint for action: Achieving center-based change through staff development._ Lake Forest, IL: New Horizons. (Assessment Tool #6, pp. 192-93). Reprinted with permission.

# Available from New Horizons

- *Avoiding Burnout: Strategies for Managing Time, Space, and People in Early Childhood Education*

- *A Great Place to Work: Improving Conditions for Staff in Young Children's Programs*

- *Blueprint for Action: Achieving Center-Based Change Through Staff Development*

- *Blueprint for Action: Assessment Tools Packet*

- *Workshop Essentials: Planning and Presenting Dynamic Workshops*


## The Director's Toolbox:  A Management Series for Early Childhood Administrators

- *Circle of Influence: Implementing Shared Decision Making and Participative Management*

- *Making the Most of Meetings: A Practical Guide*

- *The Right Fit: Recruiting, Selecting, and Orienting Staff*

- *Leadership in Action: How Effective Directors Get Things Done*


A Trainer's Guide is also available for each topic in the Director's Toolbox Series.  Each guide provides step-by-step instructions for planning and presenting a dynamic and informative six-hour workshop. Included are trainers' notes and presentation tips, instructions for conducting learning activities, reproducible handouts, transparencies, and a PowerPoint CD.


To place your order or receive additional information on prices and quantity discounts, contact:

## NEW HORIZONS

P.O. Box 863
Lake Forest, Illinois 60045-0863
(847) 295-8131
(847) 295-2968 FAX
newhorizons4@comcast.net
www.newhorizonsbooks.net